Stressing and Unstressing in a Tent

Stressing and Unstressing in a Tent

A Narrative Reminiscence by **STUART L. BURNS**

IOWA STATE UNIVERSITY PRESS / AMES

Stuart L. Burns is
Professor of American
Literature at Drake
University, Des Moines,
Iowa.

Drawings by
William D. Lee

© 1987 Iowa State
University Press, Ames,
Iowa 50010
All rights reserved

Composed by Iowa State
University Press
Printed in the United
States of America

First edition, 1987
Second printing, 1987

Library of Congress Cataloging-in-Publication Data

Burns, Stuart L.
    Stressing and Unstressing in a Tent.

    1. Camping—United States. I. Title.
GV191.4.B88 1987   796.54′0973   87-4211
ISBN 0-8138-1726-9

This
book
is
for
Sue,
Sheila,
Becky,
and T. J.

They lived that I might write

All the characters in this book are real. Occasionally, the names have been changed because I forgot the real ones. The incidents, however, have sometimes been distorted, exaggerated, or otherwise changed because it suited me to do so.

Contents

Stressing and Unstressing in a Tent

A Few Hundred Words to the Reader

ONE OF THE FEW BUT GREAT ADVANTAGES of the education profession is that it enables a family to do a lot of camping. For thirteen years, beginning in 1967, we annually spent sixty to seventy nights in a tent. In addition to numerous weekend outings we normally camped for the week preceding the Easter holiday or else a week in early June, then took an extended vacation from mid-July to Labor Day. Such a generous amount of vacation time was possible because we were a totally education-oriented family. The children were either infants (unwittingly) or students (unwillingly). When we purchased our first tent Sheila was five, Becky was two, and T. J. was ten months. Sue, the head of the open air kitchen, was for most of those years an underpaid domestic in the employ of her husband. Later she became officially employed part-time as a lunch teacher at the neighborhood elementary school.

Lunch teachers work only during noon hours, but they perform valuable educational services. Due to the typical lunch teacher's persistent efforts beginning school children increase their vocabularies measurably. Most children come to school lunch lines equipped to communicate on a single, ultrabasic level: "I don't like that!" Given a year of lunch instruction, over 90 percent of them progress to the point of being both grammatical and specific: "I don't like green beans; I don't like spaghetti; I don't like cobbler, tacos, hot dogs, poor boys, spinach, carrots." Lunch teachers also instruct children not to throw peas, as well as where to dump the peas they did not throw but didn't like.

The household head and future blower-up of air mattresses was also a teacher. As a professor of English at Drake University theoretically he taught only advanced students—that is, those who had already learned lunch. The profession has its disadvantages, the most important two of which are minimal salaries and the minimal enthusiasm of a segment of the student body who, regrettably, failed lunch on a lower level. But professing has one inestimable advantage—lots of time off from the classroom. A typical professor gets three weeks away from classes around Christmas, a week at midterm in the spring, and, depending upon his personal solvency, the whole or half of the three summer months.

Various options are open to the serious university professor as to how to spend these out-of-the-class intervals. He can attend professional meetings, do research, and prepare for future classes; he can stay home from professional meetings and devote his time to research and class preparation; he can attend professional meetings, pretend to do research, and prepare for future classes; he can stay home from professional meetings and pretend; or he can camp. The household head chose the latter of these many alternatives, except that during the cold December holidays he chose to pretend.

From 1967 through 1978 we camped extensively. And while our camping represented an escape from institutional education, it provided education of quite a different sort. Over the years we acquired a great deal of knowledge and information—some of it valuable, some merely interesting, some trivial and useless, but no less interesting for being so. We learned to interpret guide books and thus exercise greater wisdom in selecting campgrounds. We learned to distinguish between absolutely essential equipment; handy but not vital equipment; and equipment that merely takes up room. We learned to cope, as well as one can, with the vicissitudes of weather. We learned about the capaciousness of tents, the coniferousness of trees, and the capriciousness of the various vehicles we drove. We learned the difference between camping and using one's tent as a cheap motel substitute. We learned that much of the best recreation is either inexpensive or free. And we learned to tolerate, if not always appreciate, the various wild creatures whose territories we shared.

Some things—like covering the woodpile even if the night is clear—we learned repeatedly: once each year usually. We learned the folly of packing clothes for the trip on a hot day if one is heading for the mountains. We learned how to change a flat in almost every one of the thirty-three states in which we camped. We learned how to break camp in a three-o'clock-in-the-morning windstorm. We learned the real value of camping under large shady trees; we learned the real danger of camping under large shady trees. We learned how to cook and eat in the outdoors, in the car, in the tent, and in the rain. We learned how to keep our sleeping bags dry and how to sleep in them when they were wet. We learned, in short, enough to fill a book.

Here it is.

A Precise Grammar of Past and Present Tents

OUR FIRST TENT WAS A WENZEL. Our selection of this particular model did not, however, result from our having given serious thought to the question of what kind of tent would best fulfill the needs of a family of five. Indeed, we had not the slightest idea what our needs were. Our first tent was a Wenzel for the same reason that our first station wagon was a Nash Rambler—it was cheap. In both cases we got what we paid for.

Actually the Wenzel was the first tent we bought. The first tent we camped in was a no-name model that had probably been designed for an aide to General Custer. It had a floor and a zippered screen door but no windows. Its most memorable feature was a wooden interior center pole with four hinged arms that theoretically locked in place to keep the tent erect and taut. The device defied the combined intelligence of the two adults who tried to master it. On the one occasion when we used the tent in the fall of 1966, we spent approximately equal time setting it up and sleeping in it. What time we spent sleeping in it, we spent sleeping in it. A tent with a wooden interior center pole would have delighted Tristan and Isolde, a pole being a more effective deterrent to sexual congress than any sword could ever be.

The tent was loaned to us by a well-meaning friend, who once spent $13.00 to repair an electric iron when he could have purchased a new one for $9.98. We borrowed the tent because we too were trying to cut costs: while we wanted to watch the St. Louis Cardinals play a Labor Day weekend series with the San Francisco Giants, we did not want to pay the price of a motel.

It was a memorable weekend. Having invoked a grandmother clause, we made the trip without children. Knowing nothing about campgrounds, we made reservations at Diermann's Lake, a privately owned resort, which might more properly have been named Diermann's Potholes and which was designed to accommodate fishermen, not campers. But we were impressed with the fresh air and the sycamore trees fringing what Jake Diermann called "the lake." To top the weekend off, the Cardinals won three games, and we grilled T-bone steaks for Saturday breakfast.

Our joy was compounded by the discovery that camping was fun *and* inexpensive. Cheap, that is. Driving home that Monday night, we talked enthusiastically of buying a tent and doing some weekend family camping. If we shopped wisely, we agreed, we could probably find an inexpensive tent—perhaps one without a wooden interior center pole. We bought the nine-by-twelve Wenzel sidewall for $65 the next day—supposedly at 40 percent discount. It was the only tent we looked at. And we did not look at it until after we had bought it, brought it home, and set it up in the back yard.

But we rejoiced in our 40 percent savings and in our discovery that the Wenzel was supported by aluminum poles that attached on the outside. We had several good weekend outings that first fall and the following spring. Indeed, so thoroughly did we enjoy camping, that when the household head received a grant to spend two weeks in Milledgeville, Georgia, we decided to combine business with pleasure and sandwich the research between three additional weeks of vacation in the tent. Accordingly, we drove south from Des Moines in mid-July, with light hearts and no anticipation whatsoever that we would return six weeks later carrying a different tent. For the Wenzel sidewall died violently and prematurely ere the summer ended.

Once arrived at Lake Sinclair, a national forest campground located fifteen miles north of Milledgeville, the household head temporarily donned professorial garb and spent the better part of his time in the college library, acquiring information. Sheila, Becky, T. J., and their mother meanwhile donned more casual attire and had a much better time acquiring suntans. After two weeks the researcher shucked his necktie and the household headed north, camping along the Blue Ridge Parkway and capping the trip with a ten-day stay in Shenandoah National Park. Our final vacation week was by prearrangement to be spent in the more sophisticated environs of Philadelphia, where lived our long-time friends, Ruth and J. R. Fawley.

We drove into Philadelphia, eager to shower and show off our camping equipment. Having gone thirty days without sleeping in a bona fide bed, we pictured ourselves as direct descendants of Cooper's Deerslayer. Proud pioneers in a Wenzel sidewall, we insisted on demonstrating our camping expertise. After setting up the tent on the lawn, the household head cooked a dinner of camp stew on the Coleman stove. Later that evening, full of stew and pride, we retired to the Fawleys' spare bedroom to sleep. Only Dickens occupied the tent.

Dickens was an exuberant Labrador puppy. He was also an inquisitive and—at one point apparently—a panicked puppy. Sometime during the night Dickens ventured into the unzipped Wenzel. Later in the night Dickens exited from the tent—by way of the sidewall end. That there was no sidewall door bothered Dickens not one whit. When we awoke the next morning, we discovered that the toothy Labrador had converted the entire sidewall end into a door.

Our hosts were sympathetic. More importantly, they were covered. Most opportunely, their insurance agent was in the hospital recovering from an ulcer and was thus unable personally to adjust the claim. Acknowledging its legitimacy over the telephone, he asked what the destroyed Wenzel's value was. Sagely deciding that "value" might be construed as a legitimate synonym for "regularly retails at," the household head informed the ailing adjuster that the Wenzel was worth $108. The agent having agreed to furnish $100 toward replacement, the ex-Wenzel household adults visited a downtown sporting goods store that same day and, for that precise sum, purchased a tent that dwarfed the Wenzel and made Dickens the hero of the hour.

Without spending a cent of our own we acquired a tent with fifty-two more square feet of room, approximately one hundred and fifty more square feet of standing room, and no interior center pole. To memorialize the incident the household head later composed a eulogy to the unwittingly provident Labrador:

MAN'S BEST FRIEND

I sing the deeds of Dickens!
Without his master's kind consent
He made a most unseemly dent:
He went and rent our Wenzel tent.
The remnants left slim pickins.

Yet still we honor Dickens!
Whose nature was of playful bent,
Who needed no encouragement
To let loose feelings too long pent.
Our love for Dickens thickens.

And so, a toast for Dickens!
And for the insurance agent,
Who was most kind and diffident;
Acknowledging the accident,

He initiated repayment—
Wrote out a check for every cent.
It was not feed for chickens.

A toast, once more, to Dickens!
No damage done, we're all content;
He broke no cardinal sacrament;
His manners were not insolent;
In fact, they were quite continent;
We must not deem him negligent,
Nor violent, nor vehement;
He was, God bless him, innocent;
He merely was the instrument
Of forces much more virulent;
We're certain he is penitent,
And wishes to make settlement
For all his Wenzel ravishment.
So let us be benevolent;
He warrants not imprisonment,
Nor chastisement, nor banishment,
Nor any form of punishment;
He left no irritating scent,
Nor messed up things with excrement.
(That prospect really sickens!)

A toast! The tempo quickens!
The end result was provident;
Perhaps the deed was kindly meant,
Perhaps a boon from heaven sent.
Ensconced within our Hettrick tent,
We cheer—Hurrah for Dickens!

Our new secondhand Hettrick high wall was a canvas giant almost as big as a chicken house. Ten feet wide, sixteen long, it stood six foot six inches high at the corners and over eight in the center. With its heavy canvas floor, wide screened windows running almost the length of sides and back, plus a sun-reflective yellow roof, it was well lighted, airy, and spacious.

Unfortunately even clouds with silver linings contain rain. Bigger, we discovered, is not invariably better. Our Wenzel weighed forty pounds; the Hettrick weighed sixty-five when dry and about one hundred and fifty wet. Moreover, we soon discovered that the Hettrick high wall's walls were higher at some places than at others. Rain tended to collect on the roof if the tent was pitched on a slope. It is an eerie feeling to wake up to find the ceiling a foot above one's nose—water having drained south from the center and north from the corners, creating a water tank above one's unsuspecting head. Fortunately the canvas was sturdy, so we were never unceremoniously dumped on. But we soon learned the wisdom of considering the slope of the terrain before pitching the tent.

Considering the slope was not always possible, however. Most campsites have a designated pad—a graded area to pitch the tent on. While they were usually graded level, such sites were often too small. Erecting a ten-by-sixteen tent on a ten-by-twelve pad occasionally proved to be a frustrating experience. Not unusually we ended up with a pitched tent, the back end of which dangled over a railroad tie, perched upon a tree root or rock, or scrunched against a tree. Occasionally the challenge of pitching the Hettrick on a tree-cluttered, rock-infested, too-small site provoked the household adults into difference of opinion—indeed, into marriage-threatening arguments altogether disproportionate to matters of tent erection.

Our most interesting experience in tent pitching occurred in 1968. En route from the Black Hills to Yellowstone we stopped for the night at Bald Mountain Campground in the Bighorns. Arriving at sundown, we found nine of ten sites already occupied. The tenth was much too small to accommodate the Hettrick. But being wheel-weary, we made do. It being impossible to pitch the tent properly, we perched it instead—draping one corner of the canvas floor over a two-foot-high pine tree and securing it with a rope rather than a stake. Traditionally a layer of pine boughs is reputed to make an excellent mattress; pine boughs still attached to branches and trunk do not.

If the pad was large enough, it was invariably rectangular, which meant we could choose to situate the door only at one of the two rectangle ends. Generally the view we would have preferred was on the side. To indulge our desire for view, all too often we had to pitch the Hettrick in such a way as to invite the water tank effect in the event of rain. It always rained. Our one consolation was that while half of the tent collected water, the other half drained. Thus, even on the rainiest of days, we had plenty of standing room.

That is, we would have been able to stand had it not been for the clutter. While it may be true that cleanliness is next to godliness, it is indubitably the case that spaciousness is kin to slovenliness. An early addition to the furniture inside our Hettrick high wall was a card table with sawed-off legs. It would be a useful luxury, we innocently opined. On rainy days we could use it as a dining table; on other occasions we could store our tent gear on it and thus keep things neat. Besides, we reasoned, all that extra floor space might as well be put to use. It was a neat idea, as ideas go. This particular idea went berserk. By the end of the second summer the entire household had succumbed to "Chicken House Syndrome," an affliction from which we never fully recovered while camping in the Hettrick.

Strangers to the mores and manners of chickens might find further explanation helpful. The traditional farmstead chicken house has three distinguishing structural features: wall-to-wall windows on the south side, a roosting platform, and several rows of nesting cubicles. An ordinary hen spends the hours of darkness roosting. She spends most of the daylight hours sauntering around on the floor, moving from one congregation of gossiping hens to another. On most days, induced by sunlight pouring through the south windows, she takes a ten-minute midmorning break, climbs into a nesting box, and lays an egg. Then she rejoins her neighbors and discusses her accomplishment. Conversation is always rampant and voluble at midmorning in a chicken house.

If the farmer has provided the proper number of nesting cubicles, hens will use them exclusively. Trouble arises, however, if there are too many cubicles in proportion to the number of hens. Encountering too many options as to where to lay her egg, the ordinary hen becomes bewildered and noticeably less voluble. She begins to brood, in short. At such times she goes off sullenly and lays her egg in some secret place—usually in a corner under the roosting platform behind a mound of droppings. Returning to the group, she refuses to comment on the matter at all. Seeing a group of hens standing around in sullen silence, one can be almost certain that eggs will be scattered all over the place and that the gathering process will threaten both sanitation and sanity.

While the inhabitants of the Hettrick high wall were seldom bewildered or broody, silent or sullen, they did begin to display the other symptoms of chicken house syndrome. Perhaps it was the sunshine pouring through the large screen windows that induced us to scatter things about so indiscriminately, more likely it was the presence of too many storage options. Whatever the case, the card table with the sawed-off legs soon proved to be an inadequate storage cubicle, and the Hettrick generally resembled a disorderly chicken house.

Chicken house syndrome evolves from a basic logistical quirk in human nature. Given a great deal more space in which to store things, one finds immediate reason to carry a great many more things to store: more clothes, more flashlights, more games, more books, more pocket compasses, more pocket radios, more boxes of cough drops, kleenex, and Q-tips—in short, more stuff. There were times when we needed the pocket compass to find our way to the card table that we had placed in the tent so we could store things more neatly.

The Hettrick high wall was certainly the most memorable of the tents we owned. Over a period of six years we spent between three hundred and fifty and four hundred nights under its canvas roof. We pitched it in twenty-four states. Virginia was the Hettrick's graveyard.

We buried the Hettrick high wall at Cumberland Gap National Park in August 1973. The burial service itself cost us nothing since it was a private funeral with only the immediate family in attendance. But while the tent's demise was not costly, neither was it convenient. We would have much preferred a mercy killing at home.

An intimate family member, the Hettrick had shared all the stress and adversity encountered by its owners. In good weather it stood proudly, as roomy and durable as any chicken house. In bad weather it stood defiantly— sometimes. At other times, buffeted by wind, it tended to billow, then collapse. It collapsed in a steady wind one afternoon at Flaming Gorge, Wyoming, in 1968; in 1969 it collapsed in a momentary gust of wind one evening at Big Bay Campground near Shell Knob, Missouri; in 1972, buffeted by the "aftermath breezes" of hurricane Agnes, it collapsed in the middle of the night at Cape Hatteras, nearly smothering its inhabitants. Invariably, with each disaster, a corner of canvas would tear or a pole would bend or break. In its last years it required frequent needle- and-thread surgery.

Despite clear signs of its approaching old age we were shocked by the suddenness of the Hettrick's demise. One sunny August afternoon, supplies being depleted, we drove over the pass and through the gap to Middlesboro, Kentucky, in search of bread and beer. Actually, we drove right on through Middlesboro and into Tennessee for the beer, package sales of this product being prohibited in Middlesboro. Later that afternoon we found out why: sale of beer is prohibited in Middlesboro because the city has no usable bathrooms. All filling station bathrooms were labeled Out of Order. Prohibiting beer sales was apparently a thoughtful precaution on the part of the Middlesboro city fathers, a measure calculated to ease the strain on tourist kidneys.

Having called down curses upon the heads of all Middlesboro service station attendants, we loaded up bread, beer, and hamburger and drove back over the pass to our campground—there to discover our once-proud Hettrick now a mangled corpse, victim of an apparently brief but brutal rainstorm. One of its corner poles had snapped; another had ripped through the canvas roof, shredding it so thoroughly that even the Brave Little Tailor would have been dismayed. We viewed the wreckage, held a short, dolorous consultation, then a funeral. Wrapping the Hettrick in its own canvas, we dumped it in a nearby garbage can. As the poststorm sunshine slanted through the trees, the ex-Hettrick company stood ceremoniously by while the household head, lacking a Bible, quoted as best he could a part of the burial service from the Book of Psalms:

> Dust thou art, to dust returnest,
> Was not spoken of the soul;
> When a tent has died in earnest,
> Cast its corpse into a hole.

The words did not seem altogether correct, somehow. But the spirit of intent had been fulfilled, and under the circumstances, the Hettrick high wall deserved no better.

There yet remained the problem of how to camp without a tent. Cumberland Gap is a two-day drive from Des Moines. If we went home, we would have to spend one night "motelling it." Even as long ago as 1973 motels were not cheap; on the other hand, the household head was. Besides, we still had vacation time left. We discussed, then dismissed, the idea of buying another tent in Middlesboro. For one thing there was on this occasion no ailing insurance adjuster to provide in absentia the necessary funds. More importantly, we were unanimously agreed that no money should be spent in Middlesboro that might even remotely profit an owner of an out-of-order bathroom.

And for that matter we were not totally tentless. Becky had requested and received, for her ninth birthday in July, an orange five-by-eight Eureka mountain tent. The pup would sleep two adults comfortably or three children crammedly. But it clearly would not sleep five.

Our tent-shortage problem was solved by the outdoor kitchen administrator. We could, she suggested, fashion a makeshift shelter by draping the departed Hettrick's plastic ground cloth over a clothesline strung between two trees. The corners could be pulled taut and anchored with a rock or log, thus creating a tentlike appearance. Being open-ended, the structure might be slightly overventilated. But it would shelter its occupants in ordinary weather.

There remained one question: who should its occupants be? A whispered consultation ensued between the two household adults and accord was easily reached: the occupants should be the children. More whispering, and a strategy was devised—success would lie in the timely and persuasive use of the phrase "gets to." Without further delay the adults strung a rope and draped the ground cloth, pausing frequently to remark upon how good the structure looked, how sturdy it appeared, what an adventure sleeping in it would be. Then, during dinner the household head dangled the bait. "Who do you think should get to sleep in the new tent?" he casually asked. The bait was snapped up, the children clamored for the treat, and the adults retired smugly to the orange pup.

The next morning we struck camp and moved to Turkey Foot, a national forest campground near McKee, Kentucky. It was a gorgeous campground, shaded by enormous beech trees and featuring a rock-bedded stream inhabited by painted turtles of various and dazzling hues. We drove into town for supplies, and our sour recollections of Middlesboro were sweetened by the friendliness of McKee's citizens. Indeed, the natives of McKee were sweet people with sweet tooths. Although the local grocery had limited offerings of fresh meat and produce, it stocked sugar in abundance. Fifty-pound bags of sugar were stacked head high in double rows at the far end of each of the three aisles. The folks in McKee apparently liked a lot of sugar on their breakfast cereal—which seemed strange since cereal was another item in limited supply. But we were not about to question or belittle the eating habits of friendly folk who kept their filling station bathrooms clean and open to strangers.

For the first two days at Turkey Foot the weather, and our luck, held. On the third night it rained—a soft, gentle shower of the kind that induces a sense of well-being when one is lying in a tent. While raindrops patter on the canvas overhead, one stays cozy and dry beneath. True to our prediction, the open-ended plastic slantwall sheltered the children from the rain. It also sheltered a thousand or so mosquitoes, which swarmed in out of the dampness. From this point on only the advantage of size and the tradition of authority enabled the adults to maintain possession of the orange pup tent. Indeed, occupancy of the open-faced slantwall ceased after that night. For the remainder of the trip the children slept in the Ford wagon.

Having returned to Des Moines, we immediately began looking for a replacement tent. This time we determined to research the matter thoroughly and purchase the ideal tent for our needs—something cheap, we hoped. We also agreed that we no longer needed a tent the size of a chicken house. It seemed more sensible to buy an adults-only tent and farm the children out in pups. Eventually we found what we wanted; and by mid-September 1973 we had officially become a Eureka Draw-tite household.

In terms of engineering, the Draw-tite was a model of simplicity. A number of interchangeable poles interlocked to form a buffalo-hump-shaped frame from which the canvas was suspended and secured by stretch ropes. Considerably smaller than the Hettrick, its floor space measured seven by nine; and its ceiling—less than six feet at the peak of the hump—precluded comfortable standing. But it weighed only thirty-two pounds, drained perfectly, and could be set up by one person in less than five minutes.

Its primary virtue was also its major flaw: both the floor and a twelve-inch strip around the sides were constructed of a totally waterproof plastic substance. The floor inside remained perfectly dry even if the tent was sitting in a puddle. But if nothing could seep in, neither could anything seep out. A spilled coke or beer simply ran to the nearest low spot and puddled. Later, when a side seam developed an unlocatable leak, we woke up empuddled every time it rained. If seam sealing products were on the market then, we were unaware of them. Instead we bought a big sponge and consoled ourselves with the thought that nothing is ever perfect. Certainly nothing we ever bought was.

In May 1974 we bought a second Eureka pup tent, and for the next four years we were a satisfied three-Eureka household. That first summer we circled Lake Superior. In 1975 we returned to New England, stopping en route to visit once again with the Fawleys, in Philadelphia. We did not, however, set up the Draw-tite on their lawn. Although they no longer had a dog, neither did their insurance adjuster have an ulcer. So we played it safe. In 1976 we camped in the Ouachita mountains in Arkansas; then, the following year circled through Nebraska, Colorado, Wyoming, and South Dakota. By this time we had acquired a dog; but fortunately, she did not dine on canvas.

Unlike our other tents the Draw-tite died unobtrusively in midwinter. By the time we discovered it was ailing, it was already a corpse. In late May 1978 Becky invited friends to a backyard slumber party. Since it was a sizable party, she decided to set up the Draw-tite in addition to her orange pup. To our consternation we found the tent in shreds, looking much as had the Wenzel after Dickens had dined on it. But since the Draw-tite had been stored all winter, our dog was clearly blameless. Apparently it had succumbed to mildew. Who had stored it wet? In public session each household member vigorously denied all responsibility for the tent's winter dissipation. Thus the blame remained unassigned.

Vacation time approached, finding us without a major tent, hence without a viable household name. Checking at the local camp store, we discovered that the price of Eurekas had almost doubled. Further research convinced us that a cheap new tent would be about as easy to find as would a free lunch or a five-cent cigar. But after all, we recalled, the Hettrick was secondhand; and it had lasted longer than any other we owned. Furthermore it had died in harness. We thought fleetingly of driving to Philadelphia in search of another bargain but abandoned the idea, remembering the parable of the thirteen-dollar electric iron. Obviously we needed to find an inexpensive tent nearer home.

As was the case with the dog-slain Wenzel, fortune followed disaster. At a cocktail party some weeks later we learned that Larry and Verna Landis—good friends and longtime weekend camping companions—were giving up the pastime. Would they consider selling their ten-by-ten Sears umbrella? They would. Indeed, Larry offered us a package—tent, stove, grub box, and dining canopy—all for a price that restored the household head's belief in free lunches and five-cent cigars. Without hesitation we rejoiced, paid cash, and became a Sears umbrella household.

As such we remain. After 1978 we did no family camping. And when we returned to the pastime in 1982, it was an adults-only proposition. As the twentieth anniversary of our first camping outing approaches, we talk of returning to Diermann's Lake—if it still exists. We could, we agree, celebrate the event by watching the Cardinals, fishing the potholes, and admiring the sycamores—meanwhile spending each night sleeping comfortably in the Sears umbrella, happily, a tent devoid of a wooden interior center pole.

Rainy
Days
and
Mondays

Among the many things that make a particular camping trip or specific campground memorable, one of the most prominent is weather—especially, rotten weather. A Polaroid shot from our 1971 trip features the hood of our Plymouth wagon strewn with soaked sleeping bags. Puddles and other soggy equipment in the foreground testify to the dampness. On the margin below the picture the outdoor kitchen head printed the title phrase, a fragment of refrain from a then-popular song. It was a dismally appropriate caption.

Anyone who camps for an extended period must expect some unpleasant weather, of course. But there *are* limits. On occasion we have discussed the weather phenomenon with our friends and fellow campers Lew and Sheila Hainlin. We agree that, should we ever tire of teaching at Drake, we could make comfortable livings as self-employed rainmakers. We would need only to move into a drought-stricken region and set up camp—everything but the dining canopy, that is—then retire for the night, leaving bird books and binoculars on the picnic table. Rain would surely fall, and local farmers or cattlemen would reward us accordingly.

One learns valuable lessons from camping in bad weather—most of which can be summarized with a formula phrase beginning, It is always better not to. . . . Occasionally one experiences bad weather unaccompanied by a clear moral lesson. But even from these experiences one learns. One learns, for example, that God is omniscient, capricious, and probably not a camper.

Our first experience with bad-weather camping occurred in June 1967 at Louisville Lakes, Nebraska, on the second day of what we planned would be a week's vacation. The trip began inauspiciously and concluded on a diminished note.

That year the household head found himself with a week's interlude between spring finals and the beginning of the university's first summer session. So we decided to camp in western Iowa at Viking Lake State Park. Our reason for choosing this campground the reader who has followed along thus far might anticipate: it was cheap. Indeed, according to our campgrounds guidebook, it was free. And free ranked even higher than cheap on our scale of values.

We left Des Moines on Monday morning—in a steady drizzle, which, we told ourselves optimistically, would soon let up. In fact it did. When we reached Viking Lake in midafternoon, the sky was clear, the grass already drying. A good omen, we thought, a portent of things to come. Within thirty-six hours we learned a valuable lesson: never put a pennyworth's trust in omens.

The weather continued fair that evening and the following day. We swam, explored the lake with a rented rowboat, then popped corn around a crackling campfire in the evening. The only fly in the ointment was our discovery that our guidebook had erred—there was a camping fee. It was a small fee, $1.00 per night, but still a fee, hence a small fly in our ointment pot of joy and satisfaction. If we were going to pay a fee, the household head argued, we might as well explore other campgrounds. Across the Missouri River to the west lay Louisville Lakes. The name sounded intriguing, but more importantly, the campground was located in Nebraska. If we moved there, we would no longer be provincial campers.

So we moved the next day, a hot, muggy Wednesday. We arrived, set up the Wenzel on a level, grassless, cottonwood-shaded site, then, hot and sweaty from our labor, we went swimming. As the afternoon waned, it got hotter and muggier, then darker. About five a rumble of thunder sent us scrambling out of the water. By the time we had gathered our towels, piled in the Rambler wagon, and completed the five-minute drive to our campsite, it was raining.

But no matter, we agreed; we would make an adventure of inconvenience. By moving the picnic table under the tent's awning, we could keep both stove and grub box dry while we cooked dinner. But even as we carried the table to its new location, we sensed the folly of our plan. Rain slanted under the awning, soaking grub box, stove, table, and the idiots standing around it. So the outdoor kitchen head was redesignated as indoor kitchen administrator. Carrying the stove into the Wenzel, she heated a can of spaghetti, a can of beans, then laid out a loaf of bread and a tub of margarine. Since we had carried our two reclining lounge chairs into the tent along with the stove, we sat and shared our meal.

This proved to be another mistake. Water began to seep through the tent floor, lured by contact with the weighted chair runners. So we folded up the chairs and stood around, glumly waiting for the rain to stop.

After a while we noticed a sizable puddle forming outside. Although it appeared harmless, we feared that should the rain continue and the puddle deepen, water might trickle into the tent through the screen door. To forestall that possibility the household head decided to ditch the tent. Donning his raincoat, he lurched out into the downpour, located the entrenching tool, and ditched the Wenzel sidewall. Third mistake! Indeed, this was an it-is-always-better-not-to error. From the vantage point of nearly

For a while we stood in the tent, watching
the puddle grow. . . . Then we stood in the
puddle and watched it. It was a shallow
puddle, no more than an inch deep;
but it was disheartening to have it
inside the tent.

twenty years' experience, we hand along, free, this entirely reliable, myth-dispelling advice: it is always better not to ditch a tent than to ditch it. If you feel compelled to follow tradition and ditch your tent, do it only when there is no possibility that rain will fall.

The traditional method of ditching is to dig a six-inch-deep continuous trench along the tent's four sides. Then, at the spot of lowest ground level, one digs a connecting trench extending away from the tent. In theory water will rush off the tent canvas into the trench, follow its course to the low spot, enter the auxiliary trench, and flow harmlessly away. In theory it seems a simple procedure. In fact it is a nightmare-inducing task in engineering, comparable in complexity to building the Brooklyn Bridge or digging the Holland Tunnel. Disaster will attend the ditcher's slightest miscalculation. If he locates the auxiliary trench in any spot other than the exact point of lowest ground level, it will not carry the water away effectively. Furthermore, if the tent is erected on fairly level ground, water will flow sluggishly through the main trench, if indeed it flows at all. In short, unless perfectly engineered, the ditch will prove ineffective.

Ditching a tent during a downpour tends to complicate the engineering. Despite this obstacle, however, the household head's initial efforts seemed successful. Beginning his ditch at the front corner where the puddle was forming, he succeeded immediately in diverting the puddle water into the trench. Having completed the main trench, he located what he thought was the lowest spot and dug the auxiliary trench, noting with satisfaction that it immediately filled with water also.

Imagine then his consternation when, returning to the front, he discovered the puddle re-forming. Rushing back to the auxiliary trench he made yet a second discovery: it was filled with water flowing the wrong way, into the main trench. Meanwhile water cascading off the canvas combined with water rushing into the trench, creating a flood. Floodwaters surged under the tent, seeking the lowest level—which was, of course, the spot where the puddle had originally formed.

For a while we stood in the tent, watching the puddle grow. Then we stood and watched it begin to trickle through the door screen. Then we stood in the puddle and watched it. It was a shallow puddle, no more than an inch deep; but it was disheartening to have it inside the tent.

Eventually we decided that if we could sleep through the catastrophe, we would not have to stand in it. So we prepared for bed. We put the children down on air mattresses in that part of the Wenzel where the lake was shallowest. If they stayed on their mattresses, we reasoned, they would remain reasonably dry; if not, not. The adults arranged themselves in the reclining lounge chairs. No one slept especially well. The household head, especially, did not sleep especially well. In the middle of the night, in the middle of a nightmare, he overturned the chair. Or, rather, he folded up the lounge chair without first getting up. Nor is that description quite accurate. Suffice it to say that the household head awoke to find himself in a puddle, supine and in the rude embrace of a partially folded lounge chair. Meanwhile the rain continued.

Morning found us thoroughly wet and just as thoroughly depressed. But the rain had stopped and the sun shone, so we took heart. We took heart, that is, until we took stock. Our bedding was soaked, we were soaked, and our grub box was soaked beyond belief. The reader will recall that the box had been moved under the awning to keep it dry. During the night, however, the flap had quit functioning as a protective awning and had become a downspout. Reasonably watertight against an ordinary shower, the grub box was not well enough constructed to withstand a downspout deluge. Only the silverware was undamaged. Everything else was a mess: cigarettes, flour, pancake mix, sugar, salt, cereal, paper towels, matches, napkins—all were more or less indistinguishable. It was not an appetizing sight.

Nor was this the campsite's sole unappetizing feature. Had we been so miserable as to feel that nobody loved us, that everybody hated us, and that we therefore might as well go and eat worms, two steps in any direction would have served. For a full half acre surrounding our site, the ground was littered with nightcrawlers, which, having emerged during the night to encounter floodwaters, had remained topside, apparently under the mistaken impression that they were on hooks, catching fish. Had we been in the mood, we could have collected in five minutes enough bait to last the summer. We were not in the mood. What we were in the mood for was another campsite with better drainage where we would not have to tiptoe through the wildlife. So we moved to a different site on the other side of the lake.

The move completed, the outdoor kitchen administrator drove into town to replace the perished perishables and to dry all clothing at the laundromat. Meanwhile the household head strung a clothesline to drape sleeping bags over. A little later, while searching for a tree limb that would double as a clothes pole, he encountered a sign mandating the prohibition of alcoholic beverages in the campground. This rule distressed the clothes-pole seeker, who was already suffering acute cigarette-withdrawal pains. Locating the park ranger, he wistfully inquired whether the sign really meant what it said. "Well, yes, it does," the ranger replied. "But it's really meant for these danged teenagers who come in here and drink and tear things apart. Just keep your drink in a cup or glass, and nobody'll bother you." Thus consoled, the household head returned to the twofold task of drying out equipment and wetting his whistle.

Our new site was grassy and unshaded. Its primary feature was its location in a remote corner, directly across the fence from a double set of railroad tracks. Freight trains passed with noisy regularity. This pleased the children immensely, and even the household head was at first pleased with the novelty. But since the nearest track was only forty or so feet away and the roadbed was elevated, one had the uncomfortable sensation of being under the wheels of each passing train. Furthermore, when a train passed, everything in the campsite rattled, including the site's occupants.

About eight o'clock it started raining again. But having finished dinner and dried our equipment, we were not overly concerned. This was a steady rain but not a cloudburst. And since the terrain was grassy and we had not ditched the tent, we calculated we would be safe from the floodwater conditions we had endured the previous night.

Whether we were completely safe, we will never know. About two o'clock the Wenzel occupants awakened to a voice intoning, "Hey you in there!" The household head's first thought was that the voice belonged to an angry revenue officer come to arrest him for having drunk his last evening beer from the bottle. Instead it was the park ranger—a brusque but not unkindly fellow, nevertheless a bearer of disconcerting news. He had just been informed, he told us, that the Platte River had overflowed its banks and that floodwaters might engulf the campground. Personally he didn't think there was any danger. Louisville Lakes had never flooded so far as he knew. Those people up to the north were all half crazy and forever finding something to fuss about. If we stayed we would probably be safe. On the other hand, if we stayed and got drowned, that would be our business, not his.

"I come and warned you like they told me to do," he concluded, his tone clearly leaving his hands washed clean of responsibility for all consequences whatsoever.

We struck the tent and left. Throwing things willy-nilly into the back of the Rambler, we tossed the children in atop the heap. Then, urging them to go back to sleep, we drove east, straining to peer through the rain-streaked windshield, fearful that the road might any minute turn into a tributary of the Platte.

A normal camping family would doubtless have given up at this point. But we had not yet camped enough to learn the valuable lesson that it is always better to cut short a trip if one's life is threatened by weather. Foolishly we vowed to continue our battle with the elements. We decided to stop for a hot breakfast, then drive back to Des

Moines—but *not* home. Instead we would camp in the local county park we normally frequented on weekends. Our equipment was soaked again, of course, the result of packing in the rain. But we could dry it once we reached Jester Park. Only if the rain continued would we cut our "vacation" short.

Unfortunately the rain stopped and the sky partially cleared. We arrived at Jester at noon, spread out our gear, and set up the Wenzel sidewall—for the fourth time in five days. The calm lasted through dinner, but by nine it was raining again—this time with an accompanying tornado watch for the area. Or so the local weatherman announced. The announcement angered the household head to the point that he quite unreasonably rebelled. Let others do what they would, he asserted; *he* was not going to participate in a tornado watch. If the tornado desired an audience, it could look somewhere else for it. If this particular tornado had his name written on the wind, it would have to wake him up to whisper it. Muttering thus wrathfully, he curled up in his bag and went to sleep, lulled by the sound of fifty-mile-an-hour winds rustling the leaves.

The children slept well also, probably under the mistaken impression that they were safe. For most of the night the outdoor kitchen head paced the tent—no mean accomplishment since, of the total nine-by-twelve area of floor space, only four feet by four feet permitted one's pacing upright. Furthermore there were four sleeping bodies underfoot. Nevertheless the kitchen head paced the floor, pausing occasionally at the tent door to peer at the clouds playing leapfrog over the trees.

We arose next morning, transformed overnight into a normal camping family. After a brief consultation we struck the tent, rolled it up, and deposited it—still dripping tornado teardrops—on the carrier rack atop the Rambler. Loading the rest of our gear, we drove home in a steady drizzle, which, we told ourselves pessimistically, would probably never let up.

Among the valuable lessons garnered from this last experience, one in particular impressed the household head as having significant domestic ramifications: although sleeping through a tornado watch is certainly less nerve-wracking than watching it, it is always better to sleep through a tornado watch when one is alone. A companion who does not desire to sleep through a tornado watch or who finds it impossible to do so may not appreciate the sleeper's seeming casualness. In later years the outdoor kitchen head has found occasion to observe that someone capable of sleeping through a tornado might display characteristics of stupidity and insensitivity in other situations as well.

Seven years later the household head was given a second chance not to sleep through a tornado, and this time he met the crisis responsibly. In June 1974 high velocity winds struck in the middle of the night while we were camped at Spring Lake, a county park near Jefferson, Iowa. On this occasion neither weatherman nor weathersigns forewarned us of danger. When we went to bed at ten, the sky was clear, the air calm, the weatherman noncommittal. We awoke four hours later, sleep disturbed by a dull roar distinctly unlike the normal night sounds of tree toads and whippoorwills. By the time we identified the sound as wind, it was upon us. Our three Eureka tents were arranged in a triangle with the doors facing inward, less than six feet apart. Even so, the roar of wind through the two oak trees overhead made communication difficult. It also made the household head's sphincter tremble.

Nevertheless, tightening his muscles, he loudly commanded the children to grab sleeping bags and run for the car. But prompted by some sixth sense, the outdoor kitchen head countermanded his instructions, ordering everyone to wait. In the ensuing pause two twenty-foot limbs fell from the oaks, crashing directly in the space between the tents and our Ford wagon. One landed squarely within the campsite, bouncing off the picnic table and the already-fallen dining canopy. It also demolished our water jug, a fact we discovered later. At the time we knew only that the sky was falling. Finally, when the tree limbs quit thrashing, we abandoned tents and bags and fled to the car, children in the lead, adults close behind, the latter having paused to zip the tents shut—a habitual but futile gesture.

Huddled in the Ford wagon, we watched the tents go down. While the Eureka pups simply collapsed and flattened out, the Draw-tite, suspended from its interlocking frame, twisted and rolled like a rabid cricket. Although we assumed it would be mangled beyond repair, we made, nevertheless, no attempt at rescue.

About an hour later we noticed vehicle lights making the rounds of the campground. Eventually a pickup approached our site. We flashed headlights to indicate we were in the wagon—although any fool could have seen we were not in the tents. The ranger in the pickup was no fool. Nor was he prone to Chicken Little–type exaggerations. "You folks might want to think about packing up," he told us. "According to the weather bureau, there's a bad storm on the way."

This middle-of-the-night packup was the most hectic of all we undertook. Neither wind nor rain had abated, and our equipment was badly scattered. In addition we had to work directly under the two oaks. It took us over an hour despite the help of a neighbor who had only a tent to throw into the back of his pickup camper. We arrived back in Des Moines about six, collapsed for a few hours, then initiated the dreary process of drying equipment and counting our losses. The latter, we discovered, were miraculously few. We had left behind only a hatchet, a flashlight, the household head's favorite brandy glass, a section of the lantern pole, and the demolished water jug—all replaceable items. With the purchase of two new stretch ropes and the judicious straightening of several poles, we managed to restore the Draw-tite to prestorm shape. Most important, no household member had suffered injury.

Our experience at Spring Lake provided little to chuckle about, even in retrospect. Nor did we learn any valuable lessons save for those of the damned-if-you-do-or-don't variety. That tents are extremely vulnerable shelters during severe windstorms was a fact we already knew. We likewise recognized the danger of camping under a tree that decides to fall or function as a lightning rod. But there exist no really viable alternatives to the risk. One can patronize commercial campgrounds and thus avoid trees altogether, of course. But if one wishes to escape tree danger completely, it seems more sensible to give up camping, move to the suburbs, and spend the weekends watching TV.

The only sure way to avoid danger is to avoid danger. For the super-cautious, safety-conscious individual I would offer this advice: do not go camping; never swim in water more than waist deep; sell your car and stay out of boats and airplanes; give up horseback and bicycle riding; always carry a first-aid kit and an extra bottle of aspirin; stop smoking and drinking; avoid all foods containing cholesterol, carbohydrates, fats, proteins, sugar, salt, pepper, or nitrites; quit your job; desert your family if you have one; then build a bomb shelter and lock yourself in, eat all food with your fingers, and play solitaire with rubber-coated, disinfected cards. Although you will probably not be happy, you may avoid injury.

While we had no rubber-coated playing cards in the summer of 1972, we certainly would have taken refuge in a bomb shelter had we been able to locate one on Cape Hatteras. Instead we settled for a motel the June evening that we have since christened "Agnes' Day."

Our original plan that summer was to camp a week or ten days in the Smokies; visit friends in Durham, North Carolina; then spend another week or so at Hatteras. But Hurricane Agnes began kicking up her heels shortly after we left home. We followed newspaper and radio reports of the storm's progress during our Smokies stay, then moved on to Durham, expecting that thereafter we would have to alter our itinerary.

But our hopes for coast camping revived while we were

visiting James and Judy Olney. According to newspaper accounts, Agnes had abandoned North Carolina and was petering out northward. Nevertheless we thought it prudent to telephone ahead and inquire about conditions. Accordingly, on the day before departure the household head phoned the park headquarters, inquiring whether the campground was open. "By all means," a cheery voice assured him. "One road is currently closed, but there is still easy access to the campground." Thus reassured, the telephone caller reported to spouse and children that "everything is fine over there." So we prepared to head coastward.

In handing along this message, the household head was guilty of a sin against which, as a professor of English and lover of words, he has long and unsuccessfully campaigned. Language, he has preached for twenty-five years to both willing and unwilling listeners, is like water—fluid and therefore deceptively shaped by the container in which it reposes. Language is, in short, primarily connotative, subjective rather than objective, symbolic, not exact. Subject to nuance, it is always in need of interpretation. Had the English prof kept his credo in mind that day in Durham, he would have thought twice before handing on such a reassuring message.

The reader will note, for example, a measurable discrepancy between the household head's original question and the "answer" he handed on. The statement that the campground is open does *not* carry with it corollary assurance that the sensible camper would want—or even be able—to camp there. That the campground is "easily accessible" skirts all explanation of why one road should be "currently closed." Moreover, a cheery voice does not ensure a cheery environment. In short, the telephone exchange did not lead logically to the conclusion that "everything is fine over there." Subjectivity and nuance had triumphed, and the fluid language had been trapped in a container shaped by wish fulfillment. The cheery official had wished to reassure the telephone caller. The caller wished to camp on Cape Hatteras and was therefore ripe for reassurance. The telephone caller, in turn, wished to reassure his family. So the entire household ended up reassured and innocent of what was in store.

But why, one asks, did the cheery-voiced official ignore the realities of weather? Why was he so positive and reassuring in the first place? Why, in the wake of a hurricane, would a park ranger on Cape Hatteras have a cheery voice at all? Extensive acquaintance with park ranger behavior over the years has helped us develop a theory that explains the phenomenon. We herewith pass it along free, for the reader's edification.

Before he can be duly certified, a ranger-candidate must enroll in a seminar entitled "Reassuring and Educating the Camper." The philosophical thrust of this seminar stems from the assumption that the ordinary camper has insufficient intelligence to cope with raw (or even semi-cooked) nature. Therefore, he must be educated regarding certain dangers and, conversely, reassured that certain anticipations he has of danger are groundless. To be specific, would-be park rangers are programmed to admonish campers never to get out of a car to feed or photograph bears; they are trained to discourage campers from hiking undesignated or unposted trails; and they are drilled to warn campers that the fire they build will probably set the entire forest ablaze. On the other hand, rangers are taught that campers generally have an inordinate fear of skunks and snakes and must therefore be reassured that such creatures are neither numerous nor dangerous. Finally, rangers are instructed always to be optimistic about the weather.

Our own experience has confirmed that the Park Service has correctly assessed the average camper's stupidity regarding animals. The ordinary camper tends to seriously underestimate the danger posed by bears while extravagantly exaggerating the potential danger of snakes and skunks. But the average camper is not nearly so pinheaded in his hiking and campfire building activities as the Park Service assumes. Hikers seldom get lost or injured on trails, and the vast majority of forest fires are caused by lightning, not by campers. The Park Service's motive for training rangers to be weather-optimists is somewhat obscure. Apparently the assumption is that any mention of rain or cold might encourage the camper's fire-building proclivities. For whatever reason, park rangers are invariably optimistic about weather and must therefore never be trusted on that subject. But not yet having learned the wisdom of distrusting cheery voices, we bade farewell to the Olneys and drove blithely east, toward the coast and toward disaster.

Signs along the way indicated that the case for confidence in coast camping had been slightly overstated. Ditches and fields were flooded; even the highway was spotted with debris left by floodwaters. But, the day being warm and the sky patterned with big, white, fluffy cumulus clouds, we drove serenely on. Arriving at the cape in midafternoon, we pitched camp, then spent an hour on the beach, collecting shells and enjoying the antics of the laughing gulls that flocked along the shore. The wind was brisk and chilly. But we assured ourselves it would subside at sunset.

As the afternoon waned, we returned to our campsite and to more ominous signs. Our dining canopy had blown down, and one of the Hettrick's corner stakes had pulled out of the sand. We reset the canopy, then turned our attention to the tent. While we were driving stakes for guy ropes, the canopy collapsed again. We left it down and began to glance uneasily at the sky. Although the big, white, fluffy cumulus clouds seemed to be moving more rapidly, no other change was discernible there. So we set about preparing dinner. The outdoor kitchen head pan-fried a meat loaf, heated succotash in a cooking pot, and dolloped a generous helping of cottage cheese on each dinner plate as an anchor against the brisk wind. In the midst of these activities the flies arrived.

Food prepared outdoors always attracts flies, of course. But this was an invasion—a plague, in fact. As a result of that experience, all household members have been inclined to view Moses more sceptically, the Egyptian pharaoh more sympathetically. Flies settled on the tent, on the household members, on the table, on the succotash. The cottage cheese looked altogether unique. Indeed, neither it nor the succotash looked appetizing. We threw them away and dined on meat loaf, which we ate standing up—or, rather, moving around—holding meat loaf in one hand, shooing flies with the other, all the while glancing with increased anxiety at the sky.

The flies, of course, were only fulfilling their heaven-appointed task. As his familiarity with chicken house interiors might suggest, the household head grew up on a farm and thus had opportunity to observe animal behavior. Animals, he noted, often anticipate sudden or drastic changes in the weather. Cows, for example, are normally placid and docile. When they begin galloping across the pasture with their tails high, it is time to head for the storm shelter. Obviously a cow is too bulky a barometer to carry camping. But flies and other loathsome insects function equally well. Anytime you notice spiders clamoring for entrance into the tent or flies mock-peppering the cottage cheese, it is time to pack and skedaddle.

Unwisely, we did not skedaddle. Indeed, we did not even discuss the possibility. Dinner once finished, no one was willing to speak and thus risk swallowing a dozen flies. Instead we stood around, mouths clamped tightly shut, shooing flies and gazing skyward at a scene that was rapidly becoming a decipherable hieroglyphic of doom. The big, white, fluffy clouds were now, like distraught cattle, galloping across the pasture of heaven, pursued and occasionally devoured by mean black clouds with swollen bellies. Meanwhile the sun had set and the wind was whipping up more stridently.

Within an hour it began raining, whereupon we retired into the tent, crawled into our sleeping bags, and prayed for a miracle that would keep the Hettrick standing. No miracle was manifest. About ten o'clock the tent came down, smothering the five of us under wet canvas. Since there were no flies in the tent, the household head could speak freely. Speak he did, calmly and in a tone only two or three octaves above normal, advising wife and children to crawl out, load whatever wind-blown equipment they could, then wait in the Plymouth. Meanwhile he would roll up bags and mattresses.

His plan did not work, of course. So thorough was the Hettrick's collapse that only the tent's occupants separated floor from ceiling. As soon as four of the occupants crawled out, the tent clamped shut like an angry oyster. Eventually the household head gave up and wormed his way out of the collapsed tent, leaving bags and mattresses inside.

Fifteen minutes later we were on the road, searching for a bomb shelter or motel. Having located one of the latter, the household head registered the party—the only time he has ever performed that task barefooted, clad only in blue jeans and pajama top. Probably it was the night clerk's first experience with squeegeeing a Mastercharge card before recording payment. Shortly thereafter we were warmly ensconced in our motel room.

We spent several hours watching TV. One local channel confined itself solely to recording wind velocity on a picture graph. Watching the screen record gusts up to seventy-five miles an hour, we consoled ourselves that the flies, at least, must be having a bad time of it. Also, we thanked our good fortune in not having encountered Hurricane Agnes in her earlier, unpetered form.

The next morning we checked out and drove to a local hardware store, where we purchased several rolls of heavy duty tape, a giant needle, and a ball of sturdy twine. Returning to our campsite, we spent the day patching canvas, straightening and taping bent and broken poles. By sundown the Hettrick was standing once more. Indeed, it continued to stand through the night, Agnes having finally petered down to a steady, nondestructive breeze. But having no desire to press our luck, we struck camp and fled inland the next day.

Most of the valuable lessons we gleaned from this experience have already been recounted or implied, but perhaps a few bear repeating. By no means trust a cheery voice. Do not be misled by vague generalizations. If a cheery voice assures you that the wind velocity on the beach is normal or the temperature inside a volcano moderate, ask for specifics. Hate flies if you must, but do not disdain their warnings. Finally, as a general precaution: always try to keep a mountain chain between yourself and any wind that has been given a name.

Breaking camp in the middle of the night is not a pleasant pastime. Furthermore, if one is pulling stakes and rolling canvas while simultaneously keeping an anxious eye out for the first crest of Platte River floodwaters or a second flurry of oak limbs, the task becomes more complicated and nerve-wracking. Yet none of these calamities caused us even to consider giving up camping as a summer avocation. That they did not deter us had partly to do with our lightning-seldom-strikes-twice philosophy. If one has narrowly escaped the jaws of a tornado or has been lashed by the scorpion tail of a hurricane, one tends to assume it will be someone else's turn next—that having paid one's dues, one will thereafter be accorded better treatment by the weather gods, who, after all, ought to be fair in their distribution of misery and catastrophe.

But there was a second, more important reason why we never thought of forsaking camping. The experiences recounted above were isolated incidents, scattered over a period of seven years. Although traumatic at the time, they constituted but five of the many nights we spent in various tents. Interspersed between were whole trips during which we enjoyed weather so favorable that we would forget to cover the woodpile at night. And since we camped for approximately eight hundred days over a twelve-year period, we probably suffered no more than our fair share of weather-related catastrophe.

Miserable weather was another matter however. And weather-induced misery is ultimately more discouraging to the camper on extended vacation than is catastrophe. Catastrophe strikes suddenly, then is gone. Misery results from an unending succession of dreary, cold, rainy days that limit the range of one's activities and induce boredom and depression. Following our retreat from Cape Hatteras, we endured ten additional days of miserable weather, first at Oconeechee State Park in Virginia, then at Jacob's Creek, a national forest campground near Bristol, Tennessee. Rain and chill plagued us. The outdoor kitchen administrator contracted a painful earache; Sheila, Becky, and T. J. all caught colds. Sweet oil, aspirin, and Coricidin bottles cluttered the picnic table.

Meanwhile the household head was too busy pondering matters of personal identity to be much affected by physical discomfort. Beginning with a dinner party in Durham, a series of incidents had left his head awhirl.

Among other artifacts in the Olney household was a monkey—a cute three-year-old of a breed slightly smaller than those that traditionally accompany organ grinders. Gertrude had been given to James by admiring Monrovian students at the conclusion of his Fulbright lectureship there two years before. Fiercely devoted to James, Gertrude readily identified with children and tolerated the attention of most adults. Sheila, Becky, and T. J. were enthralled with her. Indeed, had she not been wiser than they regarding matters of food intake, they would certainly have foundered her with their offerings of peanuts, sweets, and greens from the Olneys' garden. They spent hours bartering food and trinkets through the bars of her cage. Or, uncaging her, they played exciting games of Nerfball keepaway on the back patio.

Timid in the presence of all wild creatures larger than a deer mouse, the household head was never entirely comfortable around the monkey. Gertrude responded in kind to his mistrust. She would chatter harshly and shrink to the back of her cage whenever he approached. For his part the household head was content to keep the relationship cordial and distant. He was content, that is, until the aforementioned dinner party—when a combination of Mary, Martha, and three martinis rendered him bereft of his senses.

Mary and Martha are not the ladies' true names. The

names have not been changed to protect innocent people
however. There were no innocent people at James and Judy's dinner party. The fact is that the household head
forgot the ladies' names almost immediately after being
introduced—probably because they had harmless, inno-
cent-sounding names.

Friends of the Olneys, Mary and Martha were something more than friends to each other. Both had married
young. After a decade or so of marriage, they reassessed
their sexual roles, divorced their respective husbands, and
took up residence together. Apparently on this particular
evening this arrangement was not to their liking either.

A practicing heterosexual and firm believer that con-
tinual practice is beneficial to the practitioner, the household head has always been slightly ill at ease in the presence of overt sexual ambivalence. On this occasion he
became sicker at ease, finding himself the object around
which a domestic quarrel began to brew. For some mys-
terious reason the younger of the two ladies began to flirt
with him, fanning her companion's jealousy, and arousing
the outdoor kitchen head to indignation.

Ordinarily a reveler in flirtation directed at himself, the
household head was in this instance decidedly uncomfortable. As the evening became gayer, his discomfort increased, as did his consumption of gin. Ultimately he arrived at that state of martini-mustered euphoria wherein
he deemed himself equal to any situation. So he decided to
redirect the evening's gaiety. If he was to be the center of
attention, he decided, he would be so on his own terms.
Suiting thought to action, he put down his martini glass,
turned away from his flirtatious pursuer, and began, himself, to flirt with Gertrude—who was also an uncaged guest
at the party. Apparently considering him an unfit rival of
James Olney, her first and only love, Gertrude rudely
spurned the household head's advances. Indeed, she bit
his wedding ring, getting portions of his finger in the process. Immediately both quarreling ladies began making
much ado over the bleeding finger, even indulging in baby
talk in their eagerness to demonstrate concern. They were

abruptly shouldered aside by the household head's rightful and wrathful spouse, who declared herself "sick and tired of all this monkey business!"

"And I do mean *all*," she said, her glare encompassing the Olneys, the ladies, the monkey, and her wounded, monkey-bitten husband.

Her action put an end to the brewing quarrel, but it did not stop the bleeding nor prevent the finger from swelling painfully. So the next day James Olney drove the household head to Duke University's hospital, where a surgeon made a clean incision, removed the wedding band, and treated the wound.

The whole incident shook the wedding-bandless household head to the very roots of his being. To be quareled over by two professedly gay ladies was unsettling. But to be, in addition, spurned and bitten by a presumably heterosexual monkey, then chewed rather vigorously to ribbons by an equally heterosexual spouse, made matters more bewildering. When he was either attacked or violently wooed by Agnes a few days later, his confusion was total.

Puzzling the matter over, he eventually decided that he must possess some exotic quality of character capable of exciting females to behavioral extremes. Further, he decided he would be better off leaving that quality unanalyzed. So he dismissed the whole experience and began paying attention to the weather, whereupon he immediately became as cold and miserable as the rest of the household had been for several days.

Fortunately those ten rainy days in Virginia and Tennessee were sandwiched between three weeks of excellent weather, so our retrospective view of the 1972 trip is generally favorable, Agnes and the monkey notwithstanding. That was likewise the case in 1971, the year of the snapshot that lends its caption to this chapter's title. That summer we suffered through two-plus weeks of rainy weather which left both our gear and our spirits bedraggled. Attempting to escape the storm front, we moved from Wisconsin to Michigan's Lake Superior shore, then west and north into Minnesota. Apparently we ran the wrong way; each move found us more squarely in the storm's middle. Fortunately the weather broke on the day we made our fourth move, to Flour Lake, north of Grand Marais on the Gunflint Trail. For the last three weeks of the trip we basked in warmth and sunshine.

Fair weather attending the conclusion of both the 1971 and 1972 trips, we viewed them as experiences in intermittent misery only. But there was another reason for our patience in the face of rain and chill. By the 1970s we had a touchstone against which to measure bad weather. The touchstone trip was that of 1968—the summer we learned how truly masterful our rainmaking abilities were.

But that is a subject unto itself, deserving its own narrative segment.

Hebrews 13:8

Jesus Christ the same yesterday, and to day, and for ever.

IN THE SUMMER OF 1968 we planned a three-week joint-camping excursion with our friends Bruce and Joy Curtis. Our plan was to spend the entire period in the Teton range, and we did indeed last fifteen days in the mountains before fleeing south to the desert. That we lasted so long was primarily attributable to our youthful optimism.

For we were a youngish party of nine: four adults, aged twenty-nine to thirty-five, and five children, aged one, two, three, four, and seven. Our optimism was less explicable, but it probably stemmed from our ignorance regarding mountain weather. Each day we told each other, "Tomorrow will surely be better." Instead, tomorrow and tomorrow and tomorrow crept on its soggy pace from day to day to the last sleetfall of the recorded trip. By the time we headed desertward, we had experienced every form of precipitation known to man—spit, drizzle, rain, downpour, hail, sleet, snow. On several occasions we experienced all these in a single day.

Our plan was to rendezvous at Jenny Lake in Teton National Park on July 28, then spend the next three weeks camping in that park and in the surrounding area. Although we managed to meet on the appointed day, we did not meet at Jenny Lake as planned. Nothing after that went according to plan either. The only constant was the weather, and it was constantly awful.

For the Hettrick high wall household the trip began uneventfully. We left Des Moines midmorning on July 19, drove west and north, and stopped that first evening at Randall Dam, a serviceable but not scenic Corps of Engineers campground near Pickstown, South Dakota. Since the day had been sunny and we planned a single night stopover, we decided not to set up the dining canopy—a decision that apparently angered the mountain gods of the West.

Next morning we drove west toward Mt. Rushmore. When we reached Badlands National Monument, we consulted our watches, then the map, and decided we could afford a brief stop. After enjoying a picnic lunch, we visited the headquarters museum, explored a short nature trail, then resumed our journey.

A few mare's tail clouds floated overhead but the sun shone warmly, so we looked forward to settling into our first permanent campsite, grilling T-bone steaks over a wood fire, and relaxing after the day's drive. It was a good plan. And like most best-laid plans it ganged a-gley. Shortly after leaving the Badlands we fell in behind a convoy of wheat combines cruising along at ten miles per hour, one enormous rear wheel of each vehicle bouncing from curb to shoulder, the other jutting over the center line. Possibly they could not have pulled over enough to let traffic pass had they wished, but the driver directly in front of us, at least, gave no indication even of wishing. So, since the highway was somewhat hilly and oncoming traffic too steady to risk passing, we snail-paced behind for two hours, pretending to admire the scenery and playing interminable games of "meadowlarks vs. blackbirds"—an impromptu contest that consisted of counting birds perched on roadside fences and telephone wires.

When we reached Rapid City late in the afternoon, we

discovered that the mare's tail clouds had gathered for a convention. And like all good conventioneers they were milling around, getting more riotous by the minute. Furthermore, it was already long past dinnertime, or so the children loudly informed us. So we abandoned the idea of steaks grilled over a wood fire and ate Colonel chicken on the road. When we arrived at Deerfield an hour later, it was semidark and spitting rain. Our initiation into mountain camping had begun.

In the days that followed, the household head finally found the answer to a question he had posed in a third-grade geography class. Having read that deserts are regions where vegetation is scant due to lack of rainfall, he was prompted to ask his teacher why no rain falls in the desert. His teacher was not a geography specialist. Indeed, she, herself a recent graduate from high school, had only one major field of study—single men. In pursuit of men she was single-minded and purposeful. In pursuit of knowledge she was of no mind at all. In any event the answer she provided was "Because it just doesn't, that's why. If it rained a lot on the desert, then it wouldn't be a desert."

Although he recognized a certain logic in the answer, the would-be blower-up of air mattresses was not totally satisfied. But as years passed, his dissatisfaction gave way to adolescence, his passing interest in geography was supplanted by an abiding fascination with anatomy, and he forgot that he had ever inquired about deserts. But time occasionally rewards even the forgetful and unconcerned. In 1968 the household head discovered the answer to the question he had posed almost thirty years before: it seldom rains on deserts because the mountains nearby have hogged all the rain. "And why," a curious third-grader might ask, "are mountains such rain-hogs?" To that the household head has a ready reply: "Because they just are, that's why. If they weren't piggish, they wouldn't be mountains."

We intended to spend a week or more in Deerfield and actually lasted five days before the rain and cold became unbearable. This was our second summer trip, the first into high altitudes. Neither our clothing by day nor our sleeping bags by night were adequate for coping with mountain rain and chill. Our warmest jackets were un-lined corduroy; our sleeping bags were good for slumber parties, not for sleet. Every evening the temperature plum-meted into the thirties—or, rather, it eased down from a daytime high of forty-five. Every morning we woke up freezing. We would build a fire and huddle around it for an hour or so until we were thawed sufficiently to eat break-fast, following which we usually hiked. We hiked a lot at Deerfield, primarily because the exercise warmed us. On days too cold or rainy for hiking we drove to Mt. Rushmore to warm ourselves at the visitor center. But since sleeping there was disallowed, eventually we would have to return to our campsite, build up the fire, and huddle around it—cold, but gloomily aware that our sleeping bags would be colder. After four days of huddling, hiking, and freezing, we decided to move to Yellowstone, where the weather, we hoped, would be milder.

On the day we left, the weather changed. As we drove west, a yellow Wyoming sun beat down and the tempera-ture soared to plus–one hundred degrees. That night we camped under a clear but comfortable sky at Bald Moun-tain, a tiny forest campground high in the Bighorns. Con-tinuing west the next day, we reached Yellowstone in mid-afternoon in a steady drizzle. Finding all park camp-grounds filled, we backtracked to Eagle River, a Bridger Forest campground nearby.

We spent the next two days exploring Yellowstone by auto, gazing at the various natural wonders through rain-streaked windows, returning several times to the geyser area, fearful that the rain might have snuffed Old Faithful. When we woke to rain the third morning, we fled south, hoping for more congenial weather in the Tetons.

And we did get a three-day respite. By the time we arrived at Jenny Lake, the appointed spot for our rendez-vous with the Curtises, the sky had cleared. Finding the campground filled and being two days ahead of schedule anyway, we drove north and east from Jackson, then south up a fire road, and pitched a primitive camp in the Teton Wilderness area under the shadow of Mt. Leidy. When the Curtises joined us two days later, the fair weather was still holding. That first day we were all fast fair-weather friends. For the next fifteen days we were wet.

Our initiation into misery and squalor was gradual, since it rained only intermittently the next few days. Indeed, the beauty and isolation of the wilderness spot rendered it so attractive that we would doubtless have stayed longer despite the rain, had it not been for the mosquitoes. Each succeeding day of drizzle produced a bumper crop of those blood-thirsty creatures. They hatched by the thousands each night, rapidly passing through adolescence in the early hours after sunrise. By lunchtime they had matured, married, and mated. By their lunchtime, that is. We were usually just sitting down to breakfast when the first wave of postcoital mosquitoes struck. By day's end we were being bitten by hoary, gray-stingered great grandmothers of trillions.

So we decided to move. Having noted that the rain always came from the west, we reasoned that it might be possible to get west of the rain. If we moved to the Idaho side of the Teton range, we speculated, we would surely encounter better weather.

Accordingly, we backtracked through Yellowstone, driving cautiously to avoid collision with the begging bears that cluttered the highway. Late in the afternoon we arrived at Riverside, an undistinguished but convenient roadside national forest campground near Ashton, Idaho. Although we planned to camp but one night there, we set up a dining canopy, having become increasingly wary of leaving stoves and pans unsheltered. Luckily too, since it began raining before we finished dinner. We washed up; then, the rain having stopped, we gathered wood, built a fire, and lounged around it, eating popcorn and drinking coffee until mosquitoes drove us tentward.

It rained again that night but cleared at sunrise. Since our projected destination, Scout Mountain, was only four hours distant, we decided to delay our start, thus giving our equipment time to dry. Our start was indeed delayed. Although the tents were dry by nine-thirty, the company's adults had in the meantime gotten involved in an exhausting two-hour search for Little Kiddles.

For readers who cannot recall these toys of yesteryear, some description might be helpful. Little Kiddles were dolls the size of a large crawdad. They came packaged in bottles, apparently to make them look cute. To the household head the bottled Kiddles looked as if they were cramped and needed air. Indeed, they looked like homunculi. There were both boy and girl Kiddles and all had names. Finally, they were the in toy for small girls. Sheila, Becky, and Hilary were all under eight; each had several Kiddles.

On this particular morning the girls did not discover they had lost their Kiddles until we were packed and ready to leave. Apparently they had forgotten to bring them back to the campsite when they quit playing the night before. Where had they left them? They didn't know. Where had they been playing? Over there someplace. What had they been playing? They had been playing "house and horse."

After further interrogation the adults pieced together the scenario. Each girl was the mother of a household of Kiddles whose purpose in life was to visit their distant Kiddle cousins. Their mothers carried them a-visiting on stick horses. Unfortunately this meant that the Kiddles were lost in three separate locations, which the girls were unable to point out. All they were able to point out was that they were not going to leave their Kiddles behind. So for two hours we waded through wet grass looking for Kiddles.

Ultimately we found the midget monsters, thus preventing a tearful bout of Kiddle hysteria. T. J. and Jason, of course, were undisturbed by the tragedy. While the girls were losing Kiddles, they had been busy misplacing little cars. But having a fleet of several dozen, they treated the loss of two or three with philosophical good humor. The adults, less philosophical, would cheerfully have mislaid two or three children without regret. But children never allow themselves to be conveniently mislaid. In any event, shortly before noon, we stowed kids, Kiddles, and little cars in the back seats of the respective bigger cars and finally got under way.

Scout Mountain was a rain hog. Our hope that the clouds were carrying their loads east across the Teton range turned out to be a pipe dream and an illusion. We had one partial day of good weather out of three we spent there. On the afternoon of that day Bruce and Joy Curtis, Sheila, and the Hettrick household head took advantage of the weather and undertook a hike. After walking through meadowland for two hours, the party encountered rougher terrain—a rugged slope studded with down timber and tangled undergrowth. At this point Sheila and her father turned back, Bruce and Joy having stated their intent to climb to Scout Mountain's summit.

The return to camp involved father and daughter in a novel but nerve-tingling experience. A herd of range cattle had moved into the meadow to graze, and the hikers were forced to pass directly through it. On the whole they would have preferred hiking through a flock of sheep, cattle being both bigger and curiouser. It was unsettling to be stared at by five or six hundred Herefords, each weighing a half ton, none guaranteed housebroken or tame. But, remembering that Zane Grey portrayed cows as respecting men on horseback, the household head hoisted his daughter to his shoulders and instructed her to make appropriate horse-rider sounds and gestures. Whether the animals were cowed into docility, dumbfounded at the sight of a two-legged horse, or simply amused at the human pretense, the ruse worked, and the hikers passed safely through.

Arrived back in camp, the household head spent the waning afternoon hours trying to discourage young Jason Curtis from playing with the latch on the Coleman cooler and thus depleting the ice supply. He did not yet know that ice would be a superfluous commodity for the next week. Shortly before five o'clock a faint shout aroused the camp-site occupants. Bruce and Joy had completed their climb.

From a distance of three or four miles we could see them clearly, standing on a promontory, their figures silhouetted against a lowering blue bank of angry clouds. By the time they reached camp two hours later, it was raining.

We ate a gloomy dinner, then repaired to the Hettrick high wall to wait out the rain, eat popcorn, keep warm, and keep up our spirits. We succeeded only in eating popcorn. Indeed, we only half succeeded at that. At some point in the evening T. J. overturned the popcorn pan, scattering kernels and duds on the tent floor. There they remained, everyone feeling too cold and listless to sweep them up. By ten-thirty everything was thoroughly soaked: water ran in diagonal rivulets across the floor and our spirits were similarly dampened. Shortly thereafter the Curtises departed to their own tent, and the Hettrick household members lay down midst water and popcorn and spent the night twisting and turning in their sleeping bags.

It was raining when we awoke, rained intermittently throughout the day and always hardest at mealtimes. By evening we were thoroughly wet, thoroughly disgruntled, and thoroughly resolved to break camp next day. Meanwhile we repaired to the Hettrick high wall to eat Spam sandwiches and more popcorn, all the while gloomily surveying the south fork of the Scout River that meandered across the tent floor. That night the Hettrick household members gave up and slept in the Plymouth wagon. Although slightly crowded and a bit odoriferous, we thereby avoided the risk of drowning in the Scout River.

Although everyone considered the river a nuisance, we were all too miserable and mind-benumbed to ask what caused it. Yet the flood could easily have been avoided had we observed one elementary principle of tent construction: the plastic ground cloth should always be slightly smaller than the tent. Water draining off the tent onto a protruding ground cloth will necessarily flow atop the cloth under the tent, thus to be ferried up through the tent floor. Conversely, water draining from the tent onto the ground will run under the recessed ground cloth, which thereby protects the tent floor, keeping it dry. Once recognized, the principle seems self-evident, so lucidly self-evident, indeed, that when we finally perceived it, we felt unabashedly stupid. But as years passed we felt better as we noticed numerous otherwise sane and capable tent campers making the same mistake. Although we never openly laughed at these strangers who turned their protective ground cloths into open-faced waterbeds under the tent floor, neither did we share our discovery with them.

Lest the reader think harshly of us for our reticence, I should add that we had reasons for not sharing the gospel of the small ground cloth. For one thing it consoled us to know that we were not the only stupid jackasses in the camping world. Our other motive was less a matter of simple human nature, more principled and more admirable. We sensed that progression to an understanding of the advantage of using a ground cloth slightly smaller than the tent floor constituted a rite of passage: it was a sacred mystery completing the novice's initiation into camping maturity. Furthermore, we recognized that, as with the sacred mystery of sex, revelation truly comes through experience. Indeed, I initially had grave reservations about revealing the mystery in these pages. I do so only because I am confident that only the initiated will understand. The jackasses will continue heedlessly to spread large ground cloths.

On the morning following our restless sleep in the Plymouth wagon, we got up, stretched a lot, drank copious quantities of coffee, then rolled up our soggy equipment. Perforce restricted from shaking the dust from our sandals, we stomped our muddy feet instead, bestowing a resounding curse on Scout Mountain, traces of which may still linger in the moist air. Then we headed north, Bruce and Joy leading the way in their VW bus. Our intent was to cut east at Idaho Falls on Route 26, drive out of the green shading on our map and into the yellow or white. Our destination, in short, was the desert—some place where the soil would be parched, the cactus and sagebrush yellowed and brittle.

As the day progressed, our spirits lifted. By late morning the rain stopped and the southwestern sky changed complexion. Occasional patches of blue peeked through the masses of gray clouds scudding overhead. When we made our roadside lunch stop, we actually enjoyed a half hour of sunshine. So, still incurably optimistic, we reconsidered, agreed that the weather had finally broken and that we might therefore continue mountain camping. Thumbing through our guidebook, we noted Teton Canyon, a campground located in Wyoming, about twelve miles east of Driggs, Idaho. Rejoicing in the increasingly larger patches of blue above, we headed for the canyon, arriving in midafternoon.

We think it was probably one of the more scenic campgrounds we ever visited. The campsites were spaciously situated, some along a trout stream, others more in the open, but all well shaded by large quaking aspens. Firewood was plentiful, already cut and split by the forest ranger. On the second day the only other camping party vacated the grounds, leaving us in sole occupancy. It was a bona fide canyon, carved by the stream that coursed along the almost perpendicular south wall. The north slope was steep, forested, and unclimbable. An inviting trail pointed the way east into the unbathed, uncombed adolescent foothills that fronted the snow-capped Tetons.

At least this is the way we remember it. In actuality we got only occasional glimpses of the campground and the canyon, both being generally obscured by the clouds that poured in from the west, ricocheting off the canyon walls, bumping and nudging each other as they jockeyed for position, huddling as close to the ground as possible. For warmth, we assumed. For most of our five days there we were literally in nine clouds, never metaphorically on cloud nine. Most of our high spirits came from the brandy bottle, which we emptied in a futile attempt to create interior warmth. The woodpile turning out to be freshly cut, soggy, and sap sodden, we struggled to keep a fire going. On one occasion we even had a fire blazing but a rainstorm promptly doused it. Craving sunshine and warmth, we were repeatedly rewarded with aspen shade and chill.

Oddly enough, Sheila, Becky, T. J., Hilary, and Jason seemed relatively unaffected by the rotten weather. Seldom did they complain, much less fuss or cry. The girls played amiably with their Kiddles while T. J. and Jason, on hands and knees, ran fleets of little cars over mud and snow roads. Miserable ourselves, we marveled at their hardiness and good spirits.

Our recognition that the children could withstand any hardship we could bear led directly to our resolve to backpack into the mountains. If we rented a packhorse, we speculated, we could hike to regions beyond the clouds and thus get above the rain. In retrospect, all four adults have tacitly agreed not even to try to remember who first broached the idea. And since we all endorsed the plan, it seems irrelevant to identify the king of fools.

Logically, of course, it would have made sense to rent several horses, thus packing uptrail in comfort. But we anticipated that horse rental would be expensive, and our combined budget allowed for only twenty-dollar-a-day expenditure. And one horse would suffice, we reasoned. The children could trade off, two riding, three hiking. Since the adults would be hiking all the way, the pace would be leisurely. And if we packed only bare essentials, even with two children aboard, the horse's load would be easy, his burthen, light.

Accordingly, on the third day we drove out the Driggs road. Stopping at a stables we had passed coming in to the campground, we inquired of the owner the rental price of a packhorse.

"What you want with one horse?" he asked.

We told him.

"You know horses?" he inquired.

Bruce and the Hettrick household head both assured him that they had grown up on farms, ridden saddle horses, harnessed and driven Percherons and Clydesdales.

The stables' owner was unimpressed. "The Tetons ain't any farm," he declared. Then, sceptically, "You taking them little kids up into the mountains?"

They were hardy little kids, we assured him.

He gazed at us, then off into space, finally back at us. "Horses don't like it in the mountains," he said. "One horse won't stay. No matter how well you hobbled him, he'd get loose and come back down. No! you can't keep just one horse in the mountains."

He paused, then added quickly: "I wouldn't rent you more than one horse neither."

At the time we were disappointed by his refusal and bitterly resentful of his assessment of our horsemanship. But he undoubtedly did us a favor in vetoing our foolhardy venture. The weather in Teton Canyon was intolerable; it would have been worse higher up. And he was right, of course; the horse would doubtless have broken its tether, leaving us stranded, miles enwildernessed with all of our equipment plus five hardy little kids to pack out.

On the day following the abortion of our mountain-packing expedition, we awoke to sunshine. Few clouds, no fog. Delighted with this turn of events, we prepared a huge breakfast, then while we devoured it, planned our day's activity—a hike up Fred's Mountain.

Assembling children, canteens, cameras, and binoculars, we piled everything into the Plymouth wagon, drove several miles west on Driggs road, then turned north on an unmaintained fire road. When it petered out, we parked the Plymouth and began our hike.

Clouds immediately assembled to accompany us. Two hours later—and probably as many miles up the trail—the wrath of the gods of the Tetons descended upon us in the guise of an electrical storm accompanied by sleet and hail of near blizzard proportions. To a veteran accustomed to the landscape and local weather conditions, the storm was probably run of the mill. For our party it was a sobering experience.

Individualists all, we were semiscattered when the storm struck. Thunder and lightning unnerved us, stinging sleet reduced visibility to near zero, and there was no clearly marked trail—only a succession of slashes and clearings interlinked by an occasional mule deer path. But we managed to avoid panic. Halting frequently to consult regarding landmarks, we negotiated a safe return to the trail head.

We suffered but one minor casualty—the loss of young Jason Curtis's car seat. A lad of fourteen months, Jay was a sturdy, willing hiker. But one could hardly expect him to make the whole ascent up Fred's Mountain afoot. So Bruce strapped the car seat on his shoulders, converting it into a makeshift cradleboard in which Jay could ride in comfort, albeit facing backwards as did the Indian papeese of earlier centuries. In our rush to get everyone into the Plymouth, then to get the overloaded vehicle back onto the main road without miring down, we left the car seat behind. The loss was not discovered until three days later, by which time we had moved several hundred miles south.

After returning to our campsite, we encountered further trials. The campfire was dead and sleet encrusted, the Hettrick high wall askew and sleet laden. The left rear corner pole was dangerously bowed, and the tent sagged under the weight of forty gallons of sleet and hail on the roof. So while Bruce busied himself scraping sleet off the fire, the Hettrick household head seized a stick and proceeded energetically to scrape sleet off his tent. Unfortunately, unbeknownst to its wielder, the stick had a nail in it. Fortunately, on the other hand, the administrator of the sleet-encrusted outdoor kitchen was inside the Hettrick. When she informed the scraper—in tones conversationally strident—that water was pouring into the tent, he wisely discarded the stick, thus averting further damage.

Indeed, damage was minimal. Weight once lifted from the canvas, the corner pole regained a reasonable semblance of straightness. And the kitchen head, ever resourceful in such crises, quickly repaired the rip in the canvas ceiling with a strip of duct tape.

From the vicissitudes of that day the Teton expeditionary force garnered two valuable lessons. They learned first the folly of angering the resident gods of Fred's Mountain. Further, they learned the wisdom of always carrying a roll of duct tape. Duct tape is to the modern tent camper what baling wire was to farmer and motorist of the 1930s—an invaluable repair item. One can employ duct tape for patching, wrapping, stripping, or roping. Indeed, one can do almost anything with duct tape except eat it. For that matter, a tolerant trencherman capable of surmounting initial prejudices regarding taste will discover that duct tape, finely grated, makes an excellent substitute for crackers in holding a meat loaf together.

On the day following the sleet storm we struck camp and fled south. We camped three nights at Lake Lucerne, in the Flaming Gorge, then dipped further south to Dinosaur National Monument—both delightfully arid regions. Indeed, our two weeks of rain-induced misery were ended.

There are, however, two additional weather incidents deserving mention ere this segment of narrative concludes. Our first night at Dinosaur we managed to scrounge up enough sagebrush and mesquite twigs to build a small fire. Within five minutes a ranger came clattering down the camp road in his jeep, jerked it to a halt, then strode into our campsite to admonish us that our campfire was a menace. Fire danger was extreme, he cautioned; and while technically he could not forbid a campfire, he strongly urged us to be reasonable and extinguish it. We assured him we had not managed to keep a fire going in two weeks—that our fires invariably petered out without becoming either warm or dangerous. And indeed, the blaze expired in half an hour, having consumed our scanty twig supply. Extreme fire danger was reduced the next day by a shower that apparently had followed our scent south from the Tetons. A mere sprinkle, too insignificant to be hogged by nearby mountains, it was nevertheless sufficient to cause the ranger to cancel the daily guided nature hike. Seasoned veterans of the wetlands, we sneered at the sissies of the plains—sage bunnies frightened of a little rain.

In subsequent years Burns and Curtis adults have reminisced often and at length about that 1968 adventure.

And we always agree that we want someday to revisit Teton Canyon. Indeed, even our children remember it fondly—as the place where Sheila and Becky cadged horseback rides from a mountain-bound excursion party; where Sheila found her lucky horseshoe under a cattleguard; where, most exciting of all, the horse stumbled onto the cattleguard, caught its hoof between rails, unseated and dragged, without harm, its lady rider. To the adults Teton Canyon represents a potential hiking and fishing paradise. Given decent weather, we agree, the scenery would be splendid, and we would probably be sole occupants of the campground.

Years have passed and we have not revisited Teton Canyon. In all likelihood we never will. Located west of both the Bighorns and the Tetons, the campground is not conveniently accessible from the Midwest. Numerous Colorado and Wyoming campgrounds offer similar enticements of good hiking, fishing, and scenery. But there is an additional deterrent. Over the years we have evolved a theory synoptic with the supposition regarding sole occupancy. The theory may be stated thus: Teton Canyon being a shrine sacred to the gods of Fred's Mountain, the weather there will never be decent for nonworshippers or outsiders. Furthermore, we fear the citizens of Driggs, Idaho, votaries of the gods of Fred's Mountain, protectors of local customs and facilities, guardians of the entry road to the canyon. (Specifically, we fear the proprietress of the Driggs Cafe. High Priestess of all the Dregs, she vigorously defends the bathrooms of that establishment against defilement by children and unshaven strangers.)

On numerous occasions while we dwelled in the rain forests of the Tetons, we were assured by friendly natives—everyone but the citizens of Driggs—that we were experiencing "unusual weather for this time of year." Indeed, that was the most valuable lesson we learned: it is always wise to expect "unusual weather" on an extended camping trip and to plan ahead, the better to cope with it. Unused winter clothing can be a nuisance to tote around. But if needed for only a single day, they are worth carrying.

A Little Light on the Subject of Camping Equipment

ONE OF OUR EARLIEST MISTAKES in acquiring equipment was our purchase of a lantern pole. It would be practical, we thought, because we could hang the lantern wherever we chose yet still have it out of our way. Daytimes the lantern pole performed admirably, keeping the lantern always out of our way. At night the lantern pole became a superfluous nuisance. A lantern that is out of the way after dark is a useless lantern. If one is eating dinner after dark, the lantern needs to be on the picnic table—at least if one is eating food good enough to deserve recognition. If one is blowing up air mattresses or unrolling sleeping bags after dark, the lantern needs to be in the tent. If one is setting up the tent after dark, one needs the lantern close by, in a child's hand. Only after the lantern has fulfilled its useful functions can one safely hang it on the lantern pole.

To be fair, one must admit that a lighted lantern hanging on an out-of-the-way lantern pole after dark is not totally useless. An out-of-the-way lighted lantern will draw bugs out of the way. Moreover, night shadows make varied and fascinating patterns in a campsite; if one has no flick-

Indeed, they are worth carrying as a preventati
them home is to summon unusual weather and
companions on the trip.

A final valuable lesson occurs to me as I wi
camping in the mountains, do not assume that a
morning will necessarily herald a sunshiny day. I
to stray from your campsite, carry something wai
you currently need, stay off Fred's Mountain, ai
sunset verify what kind of day it has been.

ering campfire to cast and enhance shadows, a lighted lantern effectively substitutes. More importantly, a lighted lantern will prevent one from stumbling into the lantern pole after dark and bumping one's nose on the unlighted lantern.

We postponed purchase of the lantern pole and most other camping items that first fall (1966), partly because we thought we should try weekend camping a few times before determining what equipment we truly needed. Besides, as the household head sagely observed, it is cheaper not to buy something than it is to buy it. We had neither air mattresses nor sleeping bags to put the mattresses under that first fall. The only mattressed household member was ten-month-old T. J. But expedience, not priority, accounted for his having a comfort denied the rest. Generally when we loaded what equipment we had into the Studebaker Lark on Friday afternoon, the last thing we loaded was T. J. It was a simple matter to haul the crib mattress with him when we hauled him out of his crib.

The rest of us slept in pinned-together blanket-bedrolls. Instead of a lantern we carried a flashlight. As substitute for a water jug we threw in the kitchen mop bucket. A shelf grate from our refrigerator served as a grill. We had no cooking set, no grub box, no axe or saw. We carried only our regular around-home clothing—a grave mistake. By late September we were acutely aware that, before we camped again in the spring, we would need raincoats, warmer jackets, and sturdier shoes.

In addition to the Wenzel sidewall we bought only a tablecloth, a styrofoam food cooler, and a one-burner combination stove and tent-heater. This last purchase probably saved our lives. Even using the heater, we came perilously close to freezing under our pinned-together blankets. By the end of the fall season—that is, the morning after we almost froze—we added sleeping bags to the top of the list of absolutely essential equipment we would need before spring.

In March 1967 we purchased most of the items listed above. But a mere inventory listing would not do justice to the quaint and curious educational experiences our shopping afforded us. From the beginning we vowed that, in the important matter of purchasing camp gear, we would not be swayed by advice offered by sales clerks or other campers. We intended to learn by trial and error instead. Our method worked marvelously: we made numerous errors, suffered severe trials, and learned a lot.

Having listed sleeping bags as a top priority, we set out early to explore the market—or, more accurately, to find the cheapest product on the market. Our first mistake, of course. We bought five Wenzel bags for $6.95 each—less than half the price listed on all other models. They were not worth half that. They were half-zippered, half-warm, and half-sized. To be fair, I should add that the bags were probably not designed for outdoor camping. They were slumber bags, designed to keep an ordinary half-grown child comfortable at room temperature. Fortunately we enjoyed room temperature weather for the first three weeks of our trip as we moved south and east to Georgia. Then we moved north into the Blue Ridge Mountains, and our romance with the Wenzels ended.

We kept them for another year with even more disastrous results. That was 1968—year of our journey with the Curtises into the rain forests of the Tetons. We froze almost every night; it rained constantly; our bags got soggy; we got soggy, hence colder. However one measures it, an adult, clothed in long underwear, blue jeans, shirt, sweatshirt, and denim jacket, simply does not fit comfortably into a child's slumber bag. Ere a week had passed, we ruined the zippers and shredded the bags, sides and bottom. Returning home in late August, we stopped for one night at Timber Creek, in Rocky Mountain National Park. We awoke to discover that, during the night, a thin film of ice had formed on the surface of our undiscarded dishpan water. A like film of ice had formed on the outside of the ruined Wenzels and, inside, on the outside of the occupants' blue jeans and denim jackets. Even the children (whom we always treated harshly if they complained) complained.

Since our Wenzel tent had been eaten by the Fawleys'

dog the previous summer, the demise of the Wenzel slumber bags marked the end of our association with Wenzel equipment. The fault, of course, was ours. We bought cheap and paid dearly.

We had one further bittersweet experience involving a Wenzel slumber bag. In the spring of 1967 we camped for a weekend in Jester Park, a small county campground half an hour's drive from our home. At the time we had not yet purchased the canvas bag we later used to hold equipment stored on the Rambler's carrier rack. Instead, we tossed the clothes bag and the five Wenzels onto the rack, placed two lounge chairs on top to form a lid, then wrapped thirty feet of clothesline around the pile. While we were driving home Sunday afternoon, a Wenzel bag wriggled loose and escaped. A group in a following car honked and alerted us to what we thought then was a misfortune. For the next two hours the household head walked the ditches beside the road, looking in vain for the bag. Evidently someone had picked it up before we could return to retrieve it. In later years it afforded us pleasure to picture the thief squirming inside the bag on a cold, rainy night.

So much for the pleasurable aspects of the episode. A second consequence we would prefer to forget. Arrived in the city, we stopped that same afternoon and wasted $6.95 for a replacement, having not yet learned that it is better to rejoice over one lost Wenzel than it is to care for the ninety and nine safely at rest atop the car.

In the spring of 1969 we trashed the Wenzel bags, replacing them with longer, heavier Colemans. For the next eight years we were warm and comfortable in our adult-sized, fully zippered Coleman bags.

Indeed, the zipper design of our Coleman bags deserves further mention—nay, deserves extravagant praise. Heavy duty zippers and wide zipper bands protected us from "kidney crisis" for as long as we used the bags. Everyone knows that kidneys are light sleepers. Exposed to fresh, moist, or chill air, kidneys invariably awake and clamor to be carried outdoors about three o'clock in the morning.

If the camper has a well-zipped bag, crisis is reduced

to inconvenience. If he has an ordinary bag, his night of agony begins. First unzipping his bag, he stumbles out of the tent to answer nature's clarion call. Returning, chilled through, he snuggles into his bag and hurriedly tugs at the zipper, which immediately snags in the fold of cloth comprising the zipper band seam. Snarled in the cloth, the zipper will neither zip nor retract. The camper must extract the cloth, tooth by painstaking zipper tooth, until the whole is free. By this time it is usually morning or else the camper's kidneys have responded to the crisis by issuing another set of imperious demands.

By 1977 the linings in the Coleman bags had pretty well disintegrated, so we replaced them with backpack-designed Dupont Fibrefill bags. Although we did not know it at the time, our exemption from suffering caused by kidney crisis was ended. The Fibrefills are lighter than the Colemans, warmer, more easily rolled and stowed. They also have a narrower zipper band. Since 1977 we have saved space, slept more comfortably, and tried to hold it till morning.

Sleeping bags are more comfortable, of course, if one has a pad or mattress underneath to cushion one from the ground and from the stones and twigs that creep under the tent after nightfall. Our first air mattresses were markedly similar to our first set of sleeping bags, being both cheap and short-lived. They were purported to be made of durable plastic, but it was a Mayfly-variety of durability. The seams dividing the tubular columns being unreinforced, the mattresses soon became lumpy and uncomfortable. Leakage followed. Ere two weeks elapsed, we found ourselves daily carrying one or more mattresses to the nearest lake or stream, there to inflate and submerge it so we could locate the air bubbles marking the most recent leak.

But one must be fair to the mattresses. Cheap and shoddy as they clearly were, they would have lasted longer had it not been for human error promulgated by parental love. That first summer T. J. was a yearling, still in diapers. As all parents and babysitters knew then (in the days before disposable diapers and tape tabs), real diapers are secured by large, ugly, sharp safety pins. Since children were invented, mothers using cloth diapers have faced the problem of what to do with the pins while the soiled diaper is being removed and a fresh one put in its place. An infant that wriggles, thus coming into contact with the point end of an unsnapped pin is invariably an unhappy infant.

The safest procedure is to unsnap the pin, extract it from the diaper, then snap it again, thus rendering it harmless. But this method has one serious drawback—it doesn't work. While one is unsnapping the pin preparatory to fastening the fresh diaper, the infant wriggles off the diaper, forcing one to resnap the pin while rescuing and readjusting the infant. Et cetera, ad infinitum. To sum up: there must necessarily be an interval during diaper changing when safety pins are unsnapped and unsafe.

There are several tried but not necessarily true ways to dispose of pins during this crucial interim. One may hold the pins in one's mouth. But aside from whatever aversion one might have to the taste, the procedure has its dangers. One sneezes unexpectedly and inhales the pin. Or, momentarily forgetting, one speaks lovingly to the infant and finds tongue and upper lip pinned firmly together.

A better solution is to stick the sharp pin into some soft material. The most conveniently located soft material is, of course, the infant, but there are obvious drawbacks to that. Alert readers may by now have anticipated the cause of our air mattress leaks. Usually we changed T. J. on a sleeping bag. The mattress beneath recorded each change with computerlike exactitude.

We never solved the problem. A habit so deeply ingrained as to be performed instinctively is not easily altered. As easily might one train a cat to protect rats or bathe with a washcloth. But even after T. J. graduated from diapergarten, our air mattress problems persisted. Indeed, it is debatable whether a problemless air mattress exists. Designed with or without pillows, with wide or narrow tubular columns, with machine- or hand-sewn seams, all air mattresses share one common characteristic: they are guaranteed to spring leaks and deflate, usually in the middle of the coldest night.

If our mattresses did not deflate due to leakage, they generally would not deflate at all. On moving days it usually took longer to pack the mattresses than it took to strike the tent and load the rest of the gear. We would lie on them, stomp on them, roll them toward the opened valve. Nothing worked. Eventually we would store them half-deflated. By the time we arrived at our new site, they would be thoroughly deflated, of course—usually, as we discovered in the middle of the night, because they had sprung a leak while riding atop the car.

Blowing up air mattresses is also a time-consuming, lung-bruising business. Over the years the household head probably missed out on thirty to forty cocktail hours, being otherwise occupied as a human bellows. Anyone who regularly blows up air mattresses is guaranteed to develop a set of lungs sturdy enough to enable him to climb Mount Everest without becoming winded. He will not become winded, that is, if he carries a waterproofed foam-rubber pad to slip under his sleeping bag. If he carries an air mattress, he will never reach the summit.

Overall it took us seven years to learn that a foam-rubber pad has most of the advantages and none of the disadvantages of an air mattress. With other items we learned more quickly. In the instance of the homemade plastic dining canopy we set a record for quick perception of folly. Less than fifteen minutes after we set it up for the second time, we wrote it off as a bad investment.

Unluckily, we encountered a seemingly workable model prototype on a windless, rainy afternoon. Our picnic table being unprotected, we had to choose, whenever it rained, one of several unwelcome ways of coping with the weather. We could take the children into the tent and listen to them squabble while we waited out the storm; we could hustle the children into the Rambler wagon and listen to them squabble while we read comic books and waited out the storm; we could bundle the children into the wagon, go for a drive, and listen to them squabble while we cruised, waiting for the rain to stop; or we could go for a walk in the rain.

The latter alternative presented the one sure way of temporarily ridding ourselves of children. Children love to squabble in close quarters, especially if they are warm and comfortable and parents are around to annoy. When they are wet and uncomfortable, generally they become morose and silent and are therefore better company. So when it rained, we usually invited them to hike with us. They would refuse and, retiring to the tent, play amicably together, there being no parents around to annoy. We would hike, thankful to be rid of squabbling children. But we would also get wet and become silent and morose and distinctly childish in our behavior.

Thus it was, that ill-fated, absolutely windless, rainy Sunday afternoon in 1967, that we morosely walked the Lake Sinclair camp loop road and were invited in, out of the rain, under Stan Mauch's homemade dining canopy. It seemed a marvel of engineering. Stan had taken a twenty-by-forty-foot piece of plastic and rolled up a charcoal briquet in each corner to provide a grommet-in-reverse to attach guy ropes to. These ropes were, in turn, tied to trunks of conveniently located loblolly pines. The canopy stood seven feet high at the corners, ten in the center. Stan had cut and topped a sapling, placed one of his cooking pots upside down over it to keep the plastic from tearing, then set the pole on the picnic table. We sat under it for an hour, comfortable and dry, watching the water drain harmlessly off the plastic, and marveling at the sheer simplicity of the construction. "How much did it cost?" we asked.

"I got the plastic for $4.95 at a hardware store in Milledgeville," Stan told us. "I bought it just yesterday."

We were delighted with the prospect of keeping our campsite dry so cheaply. We should, of course, have noted that it was a windless afternoon; in addition we should have heeded that "just yesterday" phrase. Indeed, we should have scrutinized this marvel of engineering carefully and asked a number of pertinent questions about its probable stability. Instead we drove to Milledgeville on Monday and bought a twenty-by-forty-foot sheet of plastic.

A homemade plastic dining canopy has at least a hundred and fifty negative features, any one of which—recognized—would have dissuaded us from buying the plastic. Later we wondered how soon Stan Mauch became aware of the folly of his purchase. We never found out. The Mauchs broke camp on Tuesday; and since we had not yet attempted to erect our newest camping contraption, we parted friends.

The Mauchs enjoyed their canopy for at least three days. We were not so lucky. On Wednesday we broke camp also and drove north to White Pines, a national forest campground near Brevard, North Carolina. Arriving late, we found the campground almost filled. The only available site was much too treeless and public for our taste. But rain clouds threatened, so we decided to pitch camp.

We set up the Wenzel sidewall and arranged the outdoor kitchen in good order around the picnic table. Then we unrolled our new toy. Immediately the first problem presented itself: the site contained only three trees—an enormous gum that shaded the table and two small pin oaks, the latter spaced so unevenly that we would need a twenty-foot guy rope to make use of both. Although surprised by this situation, we were not unduly concerned. We could guy the fourth rope to a tent pole, we decided. But as work progressed, it became clear that we were going to have to move the canopy about ten feet out from under the gum tree to achieve some semblance of even stress on the guy ropes. This meant moving the picnic table and the kitchen gear. More surprise and some small bit of consternation on the part of the household head, who began, uneasily, to suspect that the clear white plastic contained an invisible tincture of lemony yellow.

In the process of bringing the gum tree into alignment, we disaligned the Wenzel. To achieve rectangularity, we now needed to move the tent west five feet. This seemed altogether too much trouble. We left it in place, hoping the sheer bulk of the canopy would compensate for its being unevenly guyed. Meanwhile we had forgotten the center support pole. So, leaving the canopy tied at the corners and sagging in the middle, we began scavenging for a suitable stick.

Inasmuch as it had taken several hours to get things thus far arranged, the household head had already consumed several cans of beer. Imagine his momentary surprise and consternation when he discovered, at this juncture, an empty cooler. But no matter, he reasoned; he would finish with the canopy, then drive two miles into Brevard for a six-pack. Surprise and further consternation! A neighboring camper kindly informed him that White Pines was located in a dry county. The closest package store was in Hendersonville, thirty miles distant. Clearly the citizens of Transylvania County were responsible for this inconvenience; nevertheless, the household head included the canopy willy-nilly in his malediction.

All was not calamity and gloom however. Having located a suitable pole, the household head topped it with a cooking pot, set the pole on the table thus hoisting the canopy center—and lo, the contraption stood! Then, while we stood admiring our handiwork, a young lad of seventeen strolled into our site, carrying a paper bag containing four sixteen-ounce cans of Millers. His father, the lad explained, had learned that our cooler was empty. "Dad says no one should have to be without beer the first night out," he told us. Needless to say, we were grateful. Indeed, not until the next day did chagrin begin to vie with gratitude for emotional precedence.

Although the canopy swayed, it held through dinner and for the brief period before bedtime. During dinner we made another unsettling discovery: the lowest corner of the canopy being located directly over the fireplace, we were going to have to be careful with fires. But since we had been too busy to scavenge for wood that day, we decided that problem could wait.

We never had to deal with that problem. About ten the threatening rainstorm arrived. We lay semicomfortably in our Wenzel slumber bags, listening to the rain and picturing the water draining harmlessly off the plastic. Then we listened further while a gust of wind swirled up. Then we listened to the canopy come down. This was our moment of crisis, and we met it foolishly. We got up, dressed, went outside, and put the canopy back up. Three of four charcoal grommets having ripped out, we spent a half hour refashioning and retying the guys—getting thoroughly wet in the process. Less than five minutes after we snuggled back into our bags, the canopy collapsed again. We left it down, cleared it away in the morning, and made do with the natural canopies of trees and sky for the rest of that summer.

The following spring we purchased a store-bought canopy. But once again our propensity to buy cheap resulted in a period of frustration. The cheap canopy came equipped with only four guy ropes. It resisted erection and collapsed frequently, always in wind and rain. Then we belatedly noticed that most canopies had eight supporting ropes. We also noticed that these canopies tended to stand when ours went down. By process of deduction we concluded that our canopy would be sturdier if we added four guy ropes. Later, we bought sturdier poles, which left us with only the canvas as original equipment. We were reluctant to part with it because of its unique color. Whereas the standard canopy is blue and white or blue and yellow, ours was of a single hue—the dunnish brown shade of a sun-dried cow pie. We never saw another of that color in all our camping years. Perhaps that is why it was cheap.

But to add a postscript to the Great White Pines plastic dining canopy debacle: throughout our stay there we found ourselves surrounded by extraordinarily friendly and generous people. The neighbor who gave us the bad news concerning Brevard's beerlessness invited us to dinner one evening and cooked a farewell breakfast for us the last day. A young minister, camped with his wife and mother across the camp loop road, brought us some beef stew. For two days he had simmered it off and on in a kettle suspended from a tripod over his campfire. He had cooked too much, he explained, and didn't want to carry it home. Would we accept it? We made two scrumptious meals of it.

The gentleman who saved us from beer-withdrawal that first evening staunchly refused to accept repayment the next day. He did, however, consent to share the returned beer with us, providing we would share a snack of peanuts, cheese, and crackers, which his three daughters spread out on the picnic table. He was especially persuasive in urging Sheila, Becky, and T. J. to eat.

Thus did the light begin to dawn. How had he been so quick to come to our rescue the evening before? Was there a connection between his generosity and the continuing largesse of our other neighbors? Ultimately we were able to piece the scenario together.

Any community of decent human beings tends to view innocent folly with compassion. Our neighbors, watching our plastic canopy capers, had apparently decided we were hopelessly incapable campers. So they entered upon a kindly conspiracy, caring for us in the best way they knew—with food and drink.

Ultimately we found a use for the plastic as a protective ground cloth under the tent. We also discovered that, draped over a woodpile or grub box, it provided rain protection. And, as the reader will recall, when the Hettrick high wall died at Cumberland Gap in 1973, we draped the plastic over a clothesline, thus fashioning a temporary tent. And that is the moral, of course: plastic performs usefully when laid flat or draped over something. But it is not useful as a dining canopy. Furthermore, it is always better to wait a few days before assessing the value of a new invention, the materials for which have been purchased "just yesterday."

Alas, we never managed to immunize ourselves against the impulse to purchase gadgety items. We carried a snakebite kit with us for several years, but since we never encountered a snake that had been bitten, we never found out if it worked or not. Exercising a vein of caution, we purchased five police whistles that first spring, one for each household member to wear while hiking. A whistle is undoubtedly valuable if one is hiking alone or blazing a trail. But since we tended to stay on the trail and together, the whistles became millstones around our necks. On hikes, that is. Around camp they proved invaluable, three blasts of the whistle making a marvelous dinner bell substitute.

In the midseventies the outdoor kitchen head indulged a passion for gadgetry and purchased a doodad that was supposed to light the lantern without benefit of a match. It performed that function all right, but it was not useful. On a windy evening we might waste six to eight matches lighting the lantern. Windy or not, we regularly had to flick the roller on the doodad fifteen to twenty times before it sparked. Fortunately we mislaid the doodad within a year.

One of our most valuable acquisitions was an ice pick. An ice pick transforms block ice into cubes, thus allowing the hardy camper the luxury of a highball without the expense of cubed ice. Furthermore, a ten-pound block will last twice as long as an equal amount of cubed ice. But while we bought the ice pick to save money, we did not originally buy it to avoid the expense of cubed ice. We bought it to avoid buying dishpans.

That first summer we carried a cheap styrofoam food cooler. While it kept food and drink properly chilled, it had one major flaw—no drain plug. Consequently we had to remove everything from the cooler each day in order to dump the water. Dumping water without dumping ice cubes as well is next to impossible. But since the cooler's sides tapered inward toward the bottom, an ordinary-sized block of ice would not fit in it. We solved that problem by chopping the block into smaller chunks, using our hatchet. To preserve ice splinters and keep chopped pieces clean, we chopped the block in our plastic dishpan. After we chopped up our third dishpan, we thought of the ice pick.

In 1968 we junked the styrofoam cooler and bought a fifty-four-quart capacity Coleman that had a twist-lock lid

and a drain plug. It proved to be our best camping purchase of all time. It has outlasted two tents, two stoves, and
a lantern and still cools food while retaining ice. It looks
terrible, and we have had to rehinge the lid; but it functions. Moreover, we got it at a 40 percent discount—the
only cheap item we did not end up paying dearly for. Our
stoves and lanterns were also high-quality Coleman products, but they succumbed to hard use, bad weather, and
Georgia rust. Undoubtedly they would have lasted longer
had we given them better care. When we purchased our
second lantern, we bought a carrying case for it, and it has
consequently stayed rust-free.

Primarily, however, it is in better condition because we
have used it less. While it is nice to have a lighted lantern
in the campsite after dark, it is more enjoyable to sit
around a campfire in the darkness. And seldom is a night
so dark that one cannot make one's way, lanternless, to the
bathroom. If one absolutely must have light, a flashlight is
more convenient anyway. If one is going to read, write let-
ters, or play cards after dark, one needs a lighted lantern.
But as time passed, we found it more enjoyable to use our
eyes in the daytime and our ears at night. Rustling leaves,
hooting owls, whistling trains, shrilling whippoorwills,
chorusing tree toads, croaking bullfrogs—all night sounds,
in short, seem somehow more audible and pertinent when
lights are out.

But if we used our lantern less, we never considered
taking a trip without it. There is always the occasion when
one must cook or set up camp after dark. On such occasions it is better to have a lantern handy. And if our lantern
was not always handy, still we knew precisely where to
look for it. It would be hanging in some out-of-the-way
place on the lantern pole.

Wagon Wheels

Keep on a-turnin', wagon wheels . . .

WHEN WE BEGAN CAMPING in the fall of 1966, we owned a 1959 Studebaker Lark. We had bought it used in 1964 when our 1954 Chevy Bel Aire's timing gear went kerflooey. We were driving to Chicago, there to catch a train to Philadelphia, where we planned to spend a week with the Fawleys and their dog. The timing gear exploded just outside Iowa City about eight-thirty in the morning. When it became apparent that the Chevy could not be quickly repaired, we asked the garage owner if he had a cheap used car we could trade for. He pointed to the Lark and indicated it could be had for $500. Fearful of missing the three-o'clock Chicago train, the ex–Chevy owner said, "I'll take it," and reached for his checkbook. He was forestalled by the salesman, who asked incredulously, "Aren't you even going to drive it first?" So, unwilling to disappoint him, we test-drove it, missed our train by half an hour, and arrived in Philadelphia a day late.

The Lark was a good car—the first bargain we ever owned, since the Chevy was an outright lemon. But while the Lark ran well, a single weekend camping jaunt convinced us it would never accommodate a family of five.

While a car is technically not a part of one's camping equipment, it is an indispensable transporter of such. In our case the wagons we drove played major roles in some of our most notable camping misadventures. Almost every time we traded vehicles, it was because our current one (1) signaled its unwillingness to go on a summer camping trip, (2) died in the middle of the trip, (3) gave notice of its impending retirement while on the trip, or (4) was fired for incompetence at the end of the trip. Thus while the demise of the Chevy and the purchase of the Lark chronologically precedes the era of family camping covered by this narrative, the incident so clearly set a pattern for our later vehicular experiences that it seems relevant to summarize the episode.

Actually, we continued to use the Lark as a camp wagon that first fall. And each occasion was a challenge, an education in the art of assembling and stowing gear. Despite their youth, Sheila, Becky, and T. J. occupied most of the back seat, leaving only the trunk for storage. And it was clearly too small. Certain bare-bones necessities are required for any camping trip, however brief. We regularly carried the Wenzel sidewall, blankets, the styrofoam cooler, a change of clothing for each household member, coats and sweatshirts for cool evenings, cooking utensils and silverware, the food we planned to eat, and our mop-bucket water jug. Dolls, stuffed animals, and Tonka vehicles also found their way onto the pile of gear assembled in our driveway.

We solved the storage problem by first loading the trunk full, then loading more—following which we clamped the lid down over the mass and roped it to the back bumper. Then we removed the back seat, stowing gear on the floor. Last of all we attended to the children. While the outdoor kitchen administrator opened the rear door and braced to prevent a cascade of ill-stowed gear, the household head grabbed a child, flipped it into a horizontal position, and stuffed it on top of the mass of pans, bags, and clothing. Then, cautioning it to lie still, he repeated the process twice over.

Once arrived at our campsite, we had no difficulty unloading. We merely shouted a warning to the children, opened a rear door, and watched. Occasionally we had to search for a child buried under the ensuing debris. But they soon caught on, learning to ride the avalanche safely to the ground.

But while we managed roomwise, weight was another matter. During the winter the Lark's right rear spring buckled—a sign, we speculated, that we might have overloaded it. Besides, we had purchased additional gear over the winter, and the children, having grown, would be harder to stuff. So we knew the space logistics were hopeless. We needed a station wagon.

In March the household head herded the sagging, springless Lark to a used car lot. Within an hour he was $550 poorer, but nevertheless owner of a light blue 1965 Nash Rambler wagon. Having no train to catch that day, he even insisted on test-driving it. And since the odometer registered only 40,000 miles, he congratulated himself for having gotten a bargain that would solve space and transportation problems for years to come. The Rambler committed suicide just fifteen months later.

The experience taught us several valuable lessons: that there are more lemons than bargains on any given used car lot, that odometer readings are not trustworthy, and that test-driving is unproductive and time consuming. Like singing "Blest Be the Tie That Binds," it is a formal gesture only, a prelude to the more important action of dropping money in the collection plate.

How does one drive a bargain so as to end up driving a bargain, not a lemon? For the ordinary purchaser, subliterate in the art of auto mechanics, the problem is baffling, probably hopeless. One performs the traditional rituals of course. That is, one kicks a tire or two; examines the upholstery; counts the knobs and switches on the dashboard; opens the hood and stares in bemusement at assorted hoses, wires, and cast-iron containers; finally, one takes a test drive. Throughout, the vehicle remains inscrutably immune to prognosis.

Of course, if the vehicle has already begun to turn yellow or if there are no hoses or wires under the hood, one should be wary of buying it. Beyond that, one is at the mercy of fate and of the salesman, fate's voluble assistant. If the salesman is both merciful and knowledgeable, one sometimes drives a bargain; if the salesman is inexperienced, indifferent, or inhumane, one regrets having met him. The salesman who sold us the Rambler was inconceivably inexperienced, indifferent, and inhumane.

The Rambler committed suicide one June Sunday in 1968. Returning from a week of camping at Coralville reservoir near Iowa City, we had gotten within twenty-five miles of home when we were momentarily distracted by a muffled but nonetheless authoritative thump under the hood. A moment later a wall of steam and angry water curled from under the hood onto the windshield. Yet a moment later the Rambler wagon stopped—like the grandfather clock, "never to go again." Guilt-ridden, unable to bear the stress of sustaining the lie on the odometer, it had, in that month of moons and marriages, cracked its block.

Obviously we needed another wagon from a different used car lot. So once again the household head went a-bargaining and purchased, for $750, a six-cylinder, stick-shift 1964 Plymouth wagon painted to match our dining canopy—an unimpressive brown the hue of cat vomit. Sheila, Becky, T. J., and the outdoor kitchen head all expressed disappointment with the car's color, but the household head overrode their objections. "You can always buy a car cheaper if it's a color nobody wants," he argued. "Even if the nobody that doesn't want it is us."

Its nauseating color aside, the Plymouth wagon had one serious drawback—no carrier rack on which to store our army surplus canvas bag. While its interior was roomier than the Rambler's, we needed but one weekend trip to discover that, without our canvas bag for storage, we would be as cramped as we had been with the Lark.

And since the Plymouth was a two-door, stuffing in children would be impossible.

We researched the cost of installing a regular carrier rack, shuddered, and began thinking of alternatives. Something cheap, in short. Ultimately we settled on carpentry, constructing a four-foot-square wooden box, which we mounted on ski-carrier sticks fastened to the car top by suction cups. By painting the box dark brown, we achieved a two-toned contrast with the Plymouth's diarrhea tan.

A second drawback proved more enduring. Shortly after we bought the Plymouth, its tires began to act their age. Since the spare was stored in the bottom of the well, a flat on the road necessitated our unloading all gear save that stored in the brown box. Since the box had less capacity than the canvas bag, we always had gear stored atop the spare, both in the back and in the well. Flats invariably occurred on the road.

Indeed, only once in five years did we have a camping flat while the Plymouth was unloaded. At Johnson's Lake, Nebraska, in 1970 we awoke one Sunday morning to discover the Plymouth canting to the left. Having by this time had two years' experience with on-the-road flats, we were momentarily relieved that morning. For once, we chortled, we could change the tire without stringing gear along the highway shoulder. Only after we had the tire changed and the flat securely fastened in the bottom of the well did we realize we had chortled too soon. The nearest town where we could reasonably expect to find an open service station lay fifty miles west. Since we hoped to reach the Rockies that day, it made obvious sense to load our gear and get the tire fixed en route—which meant loading gear on top of the tire. Our spare being virtually treadless, we dared not drive on it all day. What to do?

Our first expedient was ingenious but unavailing. We tried to persuade two-year-old T. J. to curl up in the tire's place in the well, thus surrendering his place in back to the tire. He selfishly refused. So we compromised, throwing the tire in back on top of all three children. Consequently,

. . . a flat on the road necessitated our unloading all gear. . . . Flats invariably occurred on the road. . . . Sheila, Becky, and T. J. learned most of the considerable profanity they know from these tire-changing experiences.

we only had to unload and load the gear once in the process of repairing the tire and restoring the spare to its proper place.

Our usual routine was more complex. Cruising along on the highway, we would hear a muffled explosion, then the Plymouth would begin to sway. Gingerly bringing the wagon to a halt on the shoulder—usually halfway up or down a hill—we would sit quietly, look at one another, and curse. Indeed, Sheila, Becky, and T. J. learned most of the considerable profanity they know from these tire-changing experiences.

After a few minutes we would get out and unload the gear. Then the household head would wrestle the spare out of the well, pausing occasionally to curse. Then he would change the tire, usually misplacing a lug or smashing his fingers in the process. Or both. In either case, he would curse—not necessarily with imagination but always with fervor. Catching his breath, he would then wrestle the damaged tire into the well. Then we would reload the gear, start the Plymouth, and drive onward, looking for a service station. Locating one, we would stop and unload the gear. Then we would watch the station attendant wrestle the damaged tire out of the well and listen to him curse, making note of any new or imaginative epithets. The tire finally repaired and the spare securely stowed, we would reload the gear for the last time, at which point we generally discovered we had forgotten to stow the lug wrench in its proper place in the well, under the spare.

During the five years we drove the Plymouth wagon, we camped in twenty-two states. We must have had at least one flat on the road in every state. Except, perhaps, in Minnesota. In Minnesota we scraped a muffler off driving a bumpy road to Cadotte Lake, a Superior National Forest campground located about forty miles north of Two Harbors. We drove back to Two Harbors, thankful that we would not have to unload and load our gear. Instead we had to unload the brown box, the Texaco station's ceiling being too low to accommodate the Plymouth and the box on the hoist. Of course we had to unload the gear from the box before removing it.

Ultimately, however, it was not the gear in the box or well but the gear under the hood that precipitated our firing the Plymouth in mid-February 1973. That winter the wagon developed a faulty thingamabob under the hood. Or perhaps the fault lay in the clutch or gearshift, not in the thingamabob. Whatever the case, the shift lever frequently locked in neutral at intersections, forcing the driver to get out, raise the hood, and jiggle a thingamabob until the shift lever unstuck. We spent many an unpleasant minute that winter, crouched under the upraised hood, struggling with the thingamabob, and listening to the horns of impatient motorists stacked up behind us.

The climax came on February 13, a subzero, windchilled evening when the shift locked and refused to jiggle free for forty-five finger-frosted minutes. During that interim we gave the Plymouth twenty-four hours' notice.

We should have continued jiggling the thingamabob while waiting for spring. Instead, on Valentine's Day we bought a 1969 red Ford Galaxy wagon from a truly heartless used car salesman. It was an enormous nine-passenger monster, whose odometer registered 73,000 miles. But it had a carrier rack, and its spare tire fit in a circular receptacle inside the vehicle but separate from the well. Thus we could get to the tire without unloading gear—an advantage, we calculated, worth perhaps 10,000 miles on the odometer.

When we had our first flat a few weeks later, we opened the circular receptacle and found it empty. After getting the tire fixed, the household head drove to the used car lot and complained to the salesman. The latter went into a back room, lugged out a tire, and deposited it in the receptacle. About a week later we had another flat, late one evening as we drove home in a snowstorm from a Drake basketball game. But Drake had won the game, and the household head was hatted and gloved, so he changed the front tire with minimal curse and mutter. Once the spare was in place, the Ford refused to move. While the back wheels spun crazily in the snow, the wagon remained wholly stationary. Only after a stranger in a Chevy pickup tried without success to push us did we begin to suspect that something was wrong. Something was. The villain of Valentine's Day had supplied a wheel and tire that would not turn if mounted on a car with disc brakes. More complaints and eventually the Ford wagon was properly a-tired.

Whether the circular receptacle was worth ten thousand extra miles we never decided. Certainly it was not so conveniently located as first appeared. To remove the spare one had to lean in at an angle, reach down, then lift the fifty-pound tire vertically out of the receptacle. A back-wrenching, knuckle-bruising business at best. All things considered, we considered the process a trade-off against loading and unloading gear.

We traded off the Ford in 1976, immediately after we returned from our summer trip. Although a sweet, gray-haired farm lady from Mulberry, Arkansas, served as catalyst to our firing the Ford, we had long before discovered that it was a work-oriented vehicle with an aversion to camping.

It revealed its anticamping bias in July 1974. Two days before our departure the mechanism that controlled the automatic rear window quit functioning. Since it quit while the window was down, we had no option to leave it unfixed. So, early Friday morning the household head drove the Ford wagon to a garage operated by the dealership he had purchased it from. Could they fix the mechanism that day? Of course, he was assured, no problem. It was a nonproblem that plagued us for six weeks. Arriving at the garage that evening at five, the Ford owner found the wagon sitting, tailgate down, window unfixed, mechanic gone home for the weekend. Furthermore, the window was sticking too far out of its casing, so the tailgate would not close.

"We should have it ready for you by Monday noon," the shop foreman stated.

"But I need it tomorrow," the owner explained.

"I'm sorry about that," the foreman replied. "But the mechanic's gone home."

"But there are other mechanics in the shop," the owner argued. "I can see them. There's one right over there."

"I'm sorry. This is a union shop. Company policy does not permit a mechanic to finish another's work."

There followed fifteen more minutes of fruitless pleading and protest; finally the Ford's owner threw a genuine conniption fit. If he had to wait until Monday for his car, he shrieked, he would spend Monday consulting with his lawyer and complaining to the Better Business Bureau. In truth he had no lawyer, and secretly he feared that the Better Business Bureau would ignore or scoff at his complaint. Nor was the shop foreman swayed by the threats. Perhaps, he suggested, the angry owner should take the wagon elsewhere to be fixed. The Ford owner agreed that this was a good idea. But how, he inquired at the top of his voice, could he drive elsewhere with the tailgate down and the window rattling in its casing?

Ultimately the two struck a bargain. The shop foreman agreed to instruct an unauthorized mechanic to jimmy the window back into its casing far enough to allow the tailgate to close. There would be no charge if the Ford owner would thereafter leave and never return, doing with Ford and window whatever he pleased—although the shop foreman had some suggestions about that too.

The result was not altogether satisfactory. To get the window to retract at all, the unauthorized mechanic explained, he would have to loosen a doodad that could not thereafter be tightened without opening the faulty mechanism. This he was not authorized to do. He could fit the window in place all right, but he feared it would jiggle. His surmise proved accurate. When the household head backed the Ford off the hoist, the window jiggled down five inches. It remained in that position all six weeks of the trip that began the next day on schedule.

Fortunately this was not a rainy weather trip, for an

amazing quantity of water can drizzle into a car through a five-inch gap of a sloping rear window. Indeed, it rained only two or three times in six weeks and never severely. This was too little rain, for an enormous quantity of dust can also sift into a car through a gaping rear window. Our gear in the back of the wagon was dust coated after the third day. By the fourth day dust was filtering into the well. Dust accumulated in the back and in the well for about a week. Then the bottom dropped out of the well, and both dust and gear dropped with it.

We were driving a bumpy forest road in Michigan's Upper Peninsula at the time. A steel horseshoe stake apparently jiggled through a rusted hole in the well, caught on a rock or bump, lodged, and ripped out the bottom, scattering pots, pans, water canteens, and horseshoes willy-nilly. Ultimately we repaired the well by fashioning a plywood false bottom. But since we were unable to bolt it down securely, it constantly jiggled and rattled. Dust and gasoline fumes now had constant access into the red Ford. And though we kept it and drove it for two more years, we did so with saddened hearts, dusty bodies, and exhausted spirits.

As I mentioned above, we fired the Ford following our 1976 trip to Arkansas. That we remember 1976 as being one of our most enjoyable summers is amazing, considering the trouble the Ford caused. It began with a flat tire the second day out. While removing the wheel, the household head sheared a lug bolt—the second on that particular wheel. But since three lugs remained, we decided to take our chances with a wobbly wheel. A few days later the automatic rear window quit working again; the window was up at the time, however, so we didn't bother to fix it. Consequently, we always had to open the rear door instead of lowering the tailgate. Shortly thereafter someone forgot to close the door securely. It came unlatched while we drove uphill, the door swung open too far, and the top hinge snapped. Thereafter it would never close tightly— one more crack for dust to filter through.

Near Hot Springs the exhaust system fell off and lay

like a mangled snake on the highway. Fortunately it was a Midas, so we got a free replacement. Indeed, for a moment we viewed this latest malfunction as a potential blessing. A new muffler, we hoped, might decrease the amount of exhaust seeping through the plywood well-bottom. Our hopes were dashed by the Midas mechanic who informed us that the fumes were coming from a cracked manifold, not from the well.

Near Fort Smith the radiator clogged and boiled over. Once flushed, it promptly started leaking, but not badly, so we left it unfixed, refilling it occasionally, or whenever the radiator steam outside the windshield became visible through the shimmering exhaust fumes within. Meanwhile, on those days when we had sense enough not to drive anywhere, we had wonderful camping.

We pink-slipped the Ford wagon in Mulberry, Arkansas, having been encouraged in that decision by a sweet, gray-haired local farm lady. While camped at Shores Lake, we drove to Mulberry for groceries one day, hoping additionally to procure some metal tent stakes, our plastic ones proving unadaptable to Arkansas's rocky soil. Having purchased bread and beer, we drove north along the main street business district, located a hardware store, and angle-parked the Ford.

Leaving Sheila, Becky, and T. J., plus a black nondenominational puppy named Thor in the car, we entered the store, searched around unsuccessfully for a few minutes, then asked the owner if he stocked tent stakes.

"I'm sorry, but I sure don't," he said. "You'll have to look somewhere else."

Meanwhile the sweet, gray-haired lady had also been looking somewhere else.

When we emerged from the hardware store, she was standing on the sidewalk in front of our red wagon. "I'm afraid you've had a little accident," she said. She was right on both counts: there had indeed been an accident, and she was very much afraid. In attempting to back out of the parking space adjacent to ours, she had forgotten one fairly basic rule: one should back straight until one's front fender clears the rear of the vehicle to the side. Apparently she had started her car, cramped the wheels, and backed up—all without looking. From back door to rear bumper the passenger side of the wagon was badly dented and partially repainted. Indeed, it was now a dappled, red and white Ford wagon.

Acknowledging guilt but protesting that she had little money, the lady asked in a quavering tone: "Are you going to sue us?" Her use of the plural prompted us to notice her companion—a short, bow-legged man in blue bib overalls with suspenders fastened over a long-sleeved woolen shirt. He was wearing high-topped work shoes and a gray ten-gallon hat. In his neat but work-worn apparel he too appeared to be an unlikely candidate for a lawsuit.

After silently surveying the dappled indentations on the Ford, he stepped forward to explain how the accident had occurred. He was not the lady's husband, he assured us, only a neighbor. The lady, recently widowed, had never learned to drive while her husband lived. That was why they were in Mulberry on this day: she had come to town to take her driver's test, and he had accompanied her.

"We sure want to do whatever's right," the lady added. "But we aren't insured."

The red and white, dappled Ford's owners had no clear sense of what would be "right" in this situation. On the one hand, it seemed obvious that a body and fender repairman would assess the damage at several hundred dollars— more than the lady could probably afford, more, certainly, than the Ford was worth. A cursory examination yielded assurance that, while the rear door was permanently jammed, there were no jagged edges inside. The wagon's youthful and canine occupants were excited but unhurt. In short, the only serious damage was to the Ford's appearance, and the vehicle richly deserved that.

Accordingly, the household head informed the distraught lady and her bow-legged companion that he would be willing to forget the whole matter if the car's alignment was undamaged and the rear wheel cleared the bashed-in fender. Hearing this, the bow-legged neighbor squatted on his hams, grabbed the fender, grunted once, and pulled the dented metal out about three inches. "Now try 'er," he said. "I think she'll clear."

Clear she did. Minutes later, we drove away amidst a shower of benedictions. "You've been right kind," the gentleman said. "The Lord bless you folks!" the lady intoned. Then, in semiunison: "We sure do presheate all you've done!"

We did not look elsewhere for tent stakes that day. Nor did we return to Mulberry again. The unlicensed, sweet, gray-haired lady was, we agreed, Mulberry's problem altogether.

Overall the experience proved more diverting than disastrous however. Sheila, Becky, and T. J. had had an adventure; the dog had gotten to bark at the lady, unreprimanded; and the adults were accorded the opportunity to do a favor without having to exert themselves **or** spend money. They were able, in short, to be both cheap and charitable. How pleasant this feeling of nobility, effortlessly achieved.

Thirty days later, returned to Des Moines, we removed our gear from the well and dusted it thoroughly. Then we red-tagged the dappled Ford, sold it to a stranger, and bought a 1973 green Dodge wagon from a neighbor who was being transferred to California. Had he been a stranger selling his Dodge in California preparatory to becoming our neighbor, we would have been better off, for the Dodge was an unmitigated lemon. It had a predilection for expensive parts and an aversion to movement. Over the winter it developed the habit of gliding up to a stop sign and halting—permanently, or at least until towed in for repair. We spent six months and $600 replacing alternators, fuel filters, carburetors, gas pumps, generators, and ignition switches before the trouble was rightly diagnosed—a quart of sweeping compound dumped into the gas tank by some prankster. In the meantime we had dumped our children's college tuition money into the Dodge.

Ultimately our insurance company reimbursed us for

half the expense, and regarding this sum as a windfall to be spent prodigally, we bought a Coleman utility trailer. *Mirabile dictu!* The trailer's carrying capacity exceeded that of the canvas bag and the station wagon well. Unfortunately we had twenty monthly payments still to make on the Dodge. We made them, grudgingly. But when we had it paid for we fired it and bought a smaller car. Thus the era of the camp wagon ended.

But the intervening twenty months had their interesting moments. In the summer of 1977 the Dodge's battery died, suddenly and absolutely, while we were touring Custer State Park, South Dakota. Custer is a large park, spacious enough for buffalo to roam, deer and antelope to play. The town of Custer was thirty miles distant, the nearest telephone almost as far. Fortunately we had stalled at a scenic turnoff, so we exchanged a few discouraging words, then waited for a tourist to whom we could appeal for help.

One passing motorist produced a pair of jumper cables, but his battery was not powerful enough to start the Dodge. Another gentleman, with a call name of Hungry Fox, offered to try locating a tow vehicle on his CB. Within minutes he contacted Redneck Charlie, who assured us that his Land Rover was strong enough to either jump or tow us.

"If it's not too far out of the way, I'll be glad to help," he said. "Whereabouts is it that you're stalled?"

"About the middle of the south loop road, here in Custer," Hungry Fox told him.

"I'm not sure I know just where that is," came the reply.

Fox repeated the instructions.

"Never heard of that park," Redneck stated.

"Good God! man," Hungry Fox shouted. "It's the biggest damned park in South Dakota! South of Rapid City. You know—where all the buffalo are."

There was a pause, then Redneck Charlie's voice crackled, "Are you puttin' me on, Fox?"

Fox assured Redneck he was not being put on.

"Well, I'm pickin' you up here about twenty miles west of Tucson," Charlie said. "Ain't that somethin'?"

Fox and Redneck conversed for several minutes more, but the Dodge household adults quit listening, rightly guessing that Charlie would consider it "too far out of the way."

When Hungry Fox left, he promised to telephone for a tow truck when he got to park headquarters. An hour later we were rescued by an Amoco station attendant with jumper cables. We followed him back to Custer, where he installed a $70 Sealtite battery and presented a "tow charge" for an additional $55.

Custer, South Dakota, exists to provide for the needs of tourists, a fact the natives apparently resent. Like the citizens of Middlesboro, Kentucky, and Driggs, Idaho, they live by observing three golden rules: Don't talk to strangers; never unlock the bathrooms; always demand cash. Until very recently Amoco dealerships across the nation accepted only company credit cards. The attendant in Custer refused to honor even an Amoco card. He wanted cash. When we assured him we were not carrying that much cash, he assured us that that was our problem. When we offered a check, he angrily refused it. "Anyone can pretend to have a bank account," he asserted.

Thus we faced the task of trying to raise cash in a town where no one trusted anything but cash. Eventually we located a bank willing to give us a cash advance on Mastercharge, and the impasse was resolved. The $70 Sealtite, incidentally, came with a lifetime guarantee and lasted a little less than eleven months. The $55 tow lasted less than an hour.

The great Custer breakdown was our last family misadventure involving an automobile—primarily because we seldom camped after that year. The children started graduating, grew more independent, acquired summer jobs. Thus the era of family camping ended.

Transportation-wise we have come full circle, owning presently a blue 1978 Chevette that is slightly smaller than the Studebaker Lark we started with. We have used it only twice—for adults-only camping jaunts to Missouri and Wisconsin. There being no children to stuff, space is now a minor consideration, especially since we have the Coleman trailer to stow our gear in. We conclude that we have finally acquired the perfect camping vehicle. Changing a tire on the road would be a breeze. We have no need for the brown box, the Chevette has no automatic rear window, and the hatchback tailgate swings up, not out. New state laws give assurance that the odometer does not lie. Recently we purchased a new battery and replaced the exhaust system.

In short, the Chevette appears equipped to make that three-month trek to Alaska that we have talked about for years. Granted, several radiator hoses are slightly worn. We have never bothered to buy a spare for the trailer, and its wheel bearings, our local garageman warned us recently, are badly worn. But surely, we tell ourselves, we should be able to make it through that one trip without serious trouble.

POSTSCRIPT: *The concluding paragraphs above were written in the fall of 1983. The Chevette died in June 1984 in the Superior National Forest, $135 distant from Grand Marais, Minnesota, 3½ hours distant by loaded logging truck. But this chapter has recounted our misadventures with used cars. Since we replaced the Chevette with a 1984 brand-new Chevy Cavalier, our encounter with the trucker, the tow-er, and the trader— the friendly folk who helped us kick our used car addiction—will be related elsewhere in this narrative.*

First Encounters of a Closed Kind

WILL ROGERS ONCE REMARKED: "I never met a man I didn't like." Apparently self-evident, the statement is actually not free of ambiguity. Did Rogers mean, as is generally assumed, that he genuinely liked and trusted his fellow man? Or was he proudly and belligerently referring to those occasions when he refused even to be introduced to someone he knew in advance he wasn't going to like? to the sceptical camper who has purchased gas in Middlesboro, Kentucky; breakfast in Driggs, Idaho; and a Sealtite battery in Custer, South Dakota, only the boastfully belligerent version is truly believable.

During our camping years we met a few people we didn't like. Generally, however, we met them in filling stations or restaurants, not in campgrounds. The vast majority of campers we met were decent and friendly folk. Indeed, over sixteen years we encountered only three truly obnoxious campground neighbors. At Lake Texarkana, Texas, in March 1970 we shared the campground one evening with a repulsive threesome—a noisome creep accompanied by a slatternly wife and sister-in-law. Setting up a

89

tattered tent nearby, they invaded our site under pretext of borrowing stove fuel. They had packed hastily, the creep explained, because his wife's parents had just kicked them out of the house. Sitting down at our picnic table, he proceeded to burden us with tales of humiliations he had suffered at his father-in-law's hands. Alternately whining and raging, he demolished a six-pack, then helped himself to our supply—punctuating his tirade by hurling his empties into the bushes, regardless of the garbage can practically under his feet. His slattern companions drank also but, more fastidious than he, left their empties on the table. More fastidious still, they regarded pit toilet seats as incubators of every dread disease. They used the floor instead, rendering the bathroom unusable to all others.

Fortunately they stayed but that one night. Snug in our sleeping bags, we listened to them load in the morning. We held our breath until we heard them drive past our site, up the loop road. Then, as the sound of tires and engine faded, we breathed more easily, got up, dressed, and went outside—to discover their tattered tent still standing.

When we left a week later, it was still standing, unattended. Much to our relief the Texarkana trio did not return. Had the terrible father-in-law welcomed them back? Had they, homeless and rejected, driven across Texas and into oblivion? We didn't care, being simply grateful that they had decided to skip breakfast.

The following year we skipped not only breakfast but morning coffee and cocoa as well in our haste to flee the campground before the metal detective emerged from his trailer. We encountered the metal detective at Bay Furnace, a campground located on Michigan's Lake Superior shore. It was a strange encounter, which lasted five days, cost about three dollars, and culminated in our presunrise departure. Prior to leaving, however, we seeded our campsite with loose change, hoping thereby to bring a little joy into the life of the metal-detector man.

The metal detective and his wife were from Flint, Michigan. Recently retired, after having worked thirty years in a factory there, the husband had sold his home and acquired a trailer, a metal detector, and lots of time on his hands. Proud of his trailer, even prouder of his metal detector, he was nevertheless an ill-at-ease camper, intimidated by shrubbery and solitude. He thirsted for company to help him play with his new toy.

He latched onto us immediately. We had barely finished setting up the Hettrick high wall when he shambled into our site, strange vacuum-sweeperlike instrument in hand. He introduced himself and offered to find our car keys in the event we might mislay them. "Two days ago," he boasted, "the people in this site lost their car keys and I found them in their tent under a pile of laundry. I found sixty-five cents too."

The outdoor kitchen administrator explained that we had not yet had time to pile up any laundry. Would he like a cup of coffee? No! the Flint ex–factory worker declared. He was done with coffee breaks. He was through with factories and jobs, and he had a metal detector. "Tomorrow," he said, addressing the children, "we'll all go out and find dropped money."

He was dismayingly true to his word. Before we finished breakfast the next morning, he strode into our site, brandishing his metal detector and accompanied by four other campground children. Sheila, Becky, and T. J. enthusiastically joined the entourage, eager to get their fair share of quarters and car keys. Pressed to go along also, the household head made a reluctant ninth to the party. Inwardly, however, he vowed to slip off at the first opportunity to the bathroom, following which he would surreptitiously disappear.

The opportunity never arose. The metal detective led the party to a remote area, far from the nearest bathroom. In a clearing he halted by a path that looked suspiciously like a deer trail. "Lots of people must have walked along here," the prospector from Flint announced. "Let's try her out and see what we come up with."

He turned on the detector, and almost immediately it began to chatter like a stitchery party hostess. Anxious to help, the children took turns holding the detector while the Flint prospector began his dig. Indeed, so enthusiastic were the aged and youthful members of the company that even the middle-aged cynic from Des Moines became temporarily deranged. He found himself holding his breath, waiting for the moment when the prospector's spade would unearth the jeweled chest some Lake Superior pirate had buried several centuries before.

Three minutes later the prospector's spade struck metal. Like magpies waiting for a sick chicken to die, the children crowded in, eager to see what the grizzled prospector had come up with. What he came up with was a twenty-pound chunk of slag.

As its name suggests, Bay Furnace had once been an ore-smelting site. Indeed, the furnace chimney still stood. Hundreds of chunks of slag and cinder lay buried in the surrounding area, and the Flint factory man's detector waxed hysterical over each piece. Between times, it pinged on a less resonant note, announcing the location of dozens of pop-top rings. As the morning waned, the children became bored and disappeared, leaving the household head, a dispirited Sancho Panza in the company of the quixotic Don from Flint, who continued energetically detecting and digging for Eldorado.

Nor was the prospector dismayed by the children's desertion. "They'll be back," he chuckled, "the minute we find something valuable." The household head was inclined to agree. The children, he suspected, *would* return the minute something valuable was unearthed. Furthermore, he was pretty sure when that would occur—on the exact moment that the Titanic steamed into New York's harbor completing her maiden voyage.

At eleven-thirty the household head pled hunger and induced his prospecting companion to return to camp. "We'll go out again right after lunch," the prospector said. "Maybe try out along the main road."

"I'm afraid I can't," the household head replied. "I promised the children I'd take them hiking this afternoon."

"Well, tomorrow morning then," the undaunted car key locater conceded.

"Well, maybe," the Iowa cynic muttered.

Sheila, Becky, and T. J. had no desire either to spare the prospector's feelings *or* to spare their father embarrassment. At lunchtime when he suggested a hike, they declined. When he told them how much fun it would be, they were unimpressed. Ultimately he was reduced to candid confession:

"I told the metal man we were going hiking this afternoon," he explained.

"Then you shouldn't have lied," Becky declared. "That's what you always tell us."

"I don't *always* tell you that," the household head protested.

"Jinx!" all three children shouted in unison.

"That's another lie," Sheila explained.

Fortunately it began to rain shortly after lunch, thus sparing the household head public humiliation for having broken the ninth commandment. But his problem remained unresolved. While he decidedly did not want to spend his vacation digging for slag, neither did he want to hurt the feelings of the Flint factory man, who so desperately wanted a prospecting companion. Ultimately he sought advice from his spouse. "If he just wanted someone to sit, drink beer, and talk, I'd be glad to do that," he grumbled.

"Then you'd be a fool," the open air kitchen head replied. "He'd just sit there with his damned machine, waiting for you to get drunk and lose your car keys."

Next morning the Flint prospector arrived just as the household was sitting down to breakfast. The blower-up of air mattresses immediately jerked out his car keys and jangled them to forewarn the metal detective that the Hettrick high wall would not need prospecting that day.

"Are you ready to go?" the factory man asked.

"Well, uh, no, I'm not," the household head replied, gesturing at the skillet filled with scrambled eggs. "We haven't eaten yet."

"That's all right, I'll wait." The dogged seeker after slag set his detector down.

"No! No! Don't do that," the household head interrupted, then paused, acutely aware that three uncompromising youthful moralists were paying close attention.

"I'm afraid I can't go with you today," the household head mumbled, peering through the transparently thin ice covering the lake of truth he was trampling on. Keenly aware that at any moment he might hear the dreaded word *jinx*, he continued lamely, "We've got a lot . . . er, uh, um, I mean, I have several things I need to do."

In the silence that followed, it became apparent that the quixotic Don from Flint finally realized that his delight in his new toy was unshared.

"Well," he said, after a pause. "I guess I'll go along then."

"Goodbye," the household head started to say, then gargled the word into a cough, not wishing to be insulting as well as unkind. The retired factory man departed; Sheila, Becky, and T. J. kept their mouths shut; and breakfast was resumed in silence.

For the next three days the household head nursed his guilt and watched the Flint factory man trying to adapt to a world in which metal detectives lead solitary lives. Each day the prospector strode manfully out of his trailer site promptly at eight, metal detector in hand. By nine he had shuffled back and disappeared inside his trailer. On the third afternoon, filled with remorse and most of a six-pack, the household head seriously considered throwing his car keys under a pile of laundry and seeking help from his neighbor. Ultimately he discarded the idea, recognizing that only a dunce or a fanatic would fail to penetrate the ruse and not wishing to know if he was dealing with either. Instead he suggested that it was time to move. Accordingly, the household members broke camp next morning, pockets emptied of change.

Having left in haste and confusion, we had no clear destination in mind. We fled west, then north, ending up late in the afternoon at Gooseberry Falls State Park in Minnesota, north of Two Harbors. From the highway Gooseberry Falls presented a breathtaking view; from the campground there was no view at all. The 125 sites were squeezed into an area approximately the size of a large rutabaga. Most of the sites were filled, and we ate dinner that evening, elbows locked at our sides, fearful of jostling a neighbor. At least 25 camping units were located closer than the metal detective had been. Somehow we had the feeling we were being justly punished.

Although we frequently camped in filled camp-grounds, we never encountered another that gave quite the impression of shopping mall congestion as did Goose-berry Falls. Conversely, we never enjoyed more continuous solitude in a public campground than we had at Deerfield. Located sixteen miles northwest of Hill City, South Dakota, on a graveled forest road, the Deerfield campground was almost brand-new when we discovered it in 1968. For five days we were the campground's sole occupants. Nor had there been many campers before us. Trees that had been bulldozed to make campsite clearings still lay where they had fallen. Indeed, the abundance of firewood was an ex-ceedingly fortunate feature of the campground since we had five days of cold, wet weather. Throughout our stay we kept a fire blazing while we were in camp. Unfortunately the fire died if we left it unattended for more than two hours. The dry pine resembled tinder, blazing rapidly, then disintegrating into ashes. Even after we discovered the art of stump-stoking, our fire-banking efforts were thwarted by the enthusiastic industriousness of the Dutchman and his son.

Apparently because the campground was so seldom used, the Forest Service had sublet the duties of attending it. Although we never saw a ranger, the Dutchman and his son appeared promptly at midafternoon each day. First they scrubbed the already spotless bathrooms. Then they cleaned the ashes out of our fireplace. Generally there were coals among the ashes—the beginnings of a bed that might have sustained a fire overnight. But the Dutchman and his son were mindlessly dedicated. Shoving the bigger logs aside, they shoveled ashes and smaller chunks into a metal container. Then they scrubbed the concrete slab with a wet broom, emptied our garbage can, and departed, carrying fire and refuse away, presumably to some tiny, smoldering dump.

On the first day their routine amused us. By the second, recognizing the value of ashes, we attempted to dissuade them from their task. The ashes were "no bother," we told them. Without even bothering to reply, they went stolidly about the task of shoveling, sweeping, and scrubbing—leaving us each day with a fireplace as spotless as the bathroom floors.

We had as little success trying to get them to talk. We did learn that they lived on a farm nearby and that they had been hired to keep the campground clean. Keep it clean they did, and once each day we built our campfire from scratch on a spotlessly clean cement slab we could have eaten from, had we chosen to. We have since wondered whether they kept their farm as spotless. Did they stalk their cows with broom and dustpan, scour stalls and feed troughs, scrub down Mrs. Dutchman's kitchen? We never found out.

In 1977 we revisited Deerfield, circling back from Colorado. The nine-year change was sobering. All the down wood was gone, twenty more sites had been added, and worst of all, the campground had been "discovered." Half of the sites were continuously filled. Cattle and mule deer—regular campground visitors in 1968—were nowhere in evidence. Moreover, increased use had necessitated the residence of a full-time ranger. Gone were the Dutchman and his son. Thankful as we were for a fireplace with ashes, we found ourselves, nonetheless, feeling strangely restless and unfulfilled. Deerfield without deer and Dutchman was just not the same.

Quite possibly we would be disappointed with Lake Chinnabee also, were we to revisit it. Certainly it is a campground rendered memorable due to the country store man who led us to it—a man whose name we never knew and with whom we exchanged a bare minimum of conversation. Yet Chinnabee and the country store man remain memorially interlocked.

It was 1967, year of our first summer trip. Our primary destination that July was Lake Sinclair, a national forest campground fifteen miles north of Milledgeville, Georgia. Not yet initiated into the benefits of casual camping, we planned an itinerary calculated to get us to Georgia on the sixth day, with one-night stands between. But we miscalculated on the fifth day. It was nearly sunset when we reached Anniston, Alabama.

According to our guidebook, Lake Chinnabee was located fourteen miles southwest on Highway 21, then twelve miles southeast on Cheaha State Park road. We drove southwest and, after about ten minutes, began looking for a roadmark but failed to find it. Ten or fifteen minutes later, certain that we had overshot our mark, we backtracked for ten miles, still without success. And since we had failed to read the odometer at Anniston, we had no idea where we were by this time, so we pulled into a crossroads grocery to ask for directions.

Entering the store, the household head found it almost deserted. Two hatted customers lounged near the cheese case, talking in low tones to the white-aproned proprietor. Approaching, the household head inquired of the group if they knew the number of the road leading to Lake Chinnabee. The two loungers shook their heads and moved away, whereupon the store's owner took his elbows off the cheese case, straightened, and brusquely asked, "What you goin' to Chinnabee for?"

"We hope to camp there," the household head responded.

The country store man squinted through the fly-specked plate glass window and across the lot at our Rambler wagon. "How you gonna camp without a trailer?" he asked.

"We use a tent," the household head explained, indicating the canvas roll atop the wagon.

There was a pause while the country store man extracted a jackknife from his pocket, opened it, and gouged at something between his teeth.

"Oh!" he said. "Camping, huh?"

Another longish pause ensued. Then suddenly and inexplicably the country store man's whole demeanor changed. Snapping the jackknife shut, he scratched his graying hair for a moment, then said: "Lake Chinnabee, huh? Let's see, that'd be about fifteen, twenty . . . " He paused again, then asked, "Where you folks from?"

"From Iowa," the puzzled inquirer after directions replied.

"I thought so," the country store man said, paused for another reflective moment, looked around the store, then addressed the world in general. "Hell!" he said. "Ain't nobody bought anything today anyway."

Untying his apron, he shrugged out of it, meanwhile turning to the loitering customers. "You fellas want something, better get it now," he said. "I'm closing this here store up early."

Apparently not wanting anything, the loiterers walked silently to the door ahead of the country store man and the puzzled would-be Chinnabee camper. Once outside, the proprietor locked the inside door, banged the screen shut, then swung around, striding across the lot toward a battered pickup parked near the Rambler. Stopping halfway, he peered at the Rambler once again, then swung around toward the store.

"Wait just a minute, young fella," he said, unlocked the door, entered, and emerged a few seconds later with a fistful of licorice twists. "Give these to the lady and the cheerdren," he said, and strode to the pickup where, standing with the door half-opened, he issued his last command.

"Just you follow me," he said. "Try to keep close."

That proved to be no easy task. Battered as was the pickup, it proved capable of Indianapolis 500 speeds. The country store man led us south three miles, then swung left on a winding blacktop. Apparently familiar with the road, he slackened speed only slightly. The outdoor kitchen head, driver of the Rambler, tried, with compressed lips and whitened knuckles, "to keep close"—lest our guide should suddenly turn into some concealed byway and lose us forever.

But there were no side roads presenting troublesome choices. After a half hour of frenzied pursuit, we surged over the brow of a particularly steep hill, from which point we spied the battered pickup crossways in the road at the bottom, in the process of turning around. Halting, we waited while the country store man gunned his vehicle up the slope. Once abreast, he braked and, leaning out of his window, shouted above the noise of his revving engine, "Chinnabee's about a quarter mile on thataway. Just follow this road straight on down."

"How much do we owe you?" the household head shouted back, recalling a ritual from his country boyhood.

"Not a thing," was the reply. "You folks enjoy yourselves now." And the battered pickup sped away, leaving us a quarter of a mile from the campground we could not possibly have missed had the country store man given directions while leaning on his cheese case.

By the time we reached the campground, it was nearly dark. There were only five sites, four already occupied. But the vacant site was ideal—located at the end of the loop, several hundred yards distant from the others. Although far from the lake, our tent pad fronted the bank of a pebble-bottomed stream. Its subdued gurgle accompanied all our afterdark activities—pitching camp, eating dinner, sleeping.

Chinnabee was our first streamside campsite and probably memorable for that reason alone. Our twilight arrival doubtless added to the romance of the place. But most of all we remember the country store man—a good samaritan, a swift and skillful guide, and, by his own assertion, a man who thought we were from Iowa even before we confessed it.

Circumstances prevented our learning the name of the Alabama good samaritan, a man with whom we exchanged fewer than a hundred words. On a later occasion we exchanged no words at all with the Baptist deacon, although we could probably have learned his name had we so chosen. In this case we chose to shun his acquaintance because he doubtless supported a crusade that led to our temporary discomfort. Still, the thought of the deacon's own probable discomfort of conscience so tickled our fancy that he remains unforgettable, even if unmet.

We were camped at White Pines, near Brevard, North Carolina—scene of the great plastic dining canopy debacle and the occasion when the household head ran out of beer in a dry county. Judging from the sounds blaring from his radio, the deacon doubtless had a hand in keeping Transylvania County dry. From his site in the center of the campground there issued a steady, high volume intermixture of hymns and moral uplift. Daily the music informed us that grace is amazing, that a king would arrive before sundown, and that somebody walked and talked with Jesus in a rose garden, doing a tolerable amount of tarrying and sharing joy. Between songs Reverend Ike held forth.

We learned about the Baptist deacon from our neighbors to the north—friendly natives who disapproved of loud radios and local option blue laws. One evening when the outdoor kitchen head commented wryly on the "Sunday school aura" of the campground, our neighbor exclaimed, "You don't know the half of that," following which he proceeded to fill us in on the half we didn't know.

The deacon, he told us, was a business acquaintance. In the early 1950s he had constructed a bomb shelter, assuming that when the Russians attacked, Brevard would be a primary target. Fifteen years later and a little less paranoid, he converted the shelter into a family room, complete with TV. Unfortunately the Baptist minister viewed television as a gadget placed on earth by the Devil to seduce man into channel-switching his way into eternal perdition. Unwilling to resign as deacon but equally unwilling to forego watching Ed Sullivan, Brevard's video-Baptist had hired a firm to install an underground cable so that his TV aerial could be erected in the forest, several hundred yards from his house. All the digging and installa-

tion had to be done at night, of course, which meant over-
time. "And I don't think he's fooled anybody," our
neighbor concluded. "I know all about it, and I'm not even
a Baptist." He paused, took a swallow of Pabst, then added,
"Thank God!"

We never asked Rex and Jerry whether they were Bap-
tists, although they certainly knew all the songs that Bap-
tists, Methodists, snake handlers, and Grand Ole Opry
stars sing. But their talent for hymn playing and singing
was not their sole memorable quality. Whenever we think
of country music, side meat, bourbon, or Kris Kristofferson, we immediately think of Burrell's Ford, South Carolina, and of the duo that made our stay there unforgettable.

In the summer of 1973 the household head was appointed a visiting professor at Georgia College in
Milledgeville, his task to teach a four-week graduate
seminar on the fiction of Flannery O'Connor. It was a flat-
tering appointment—something one should not refuse. But
it did slice four weeks off the household's summer vacation
time. The household head effected a compromise of sorts,
setting up the Hettrick high wall near a college-owned
lake. But neither he nor his family considered the month to
be a totally satisfying camping experience. Indeed, when
the household moved north to begin the "real" vacation at
Burrell's Ford, the usual sense of togetherness was
strained.

For the household head had completed professing in a
very undignified manner, having celebrated the term's
conclusion by drinking a tad too much, then—in the middle of the night—stumbling barefooted repeatedly over a
metal tent stake while trying to answer a call of nature.
Thus, on the initial real vacation day the kitchen administrator nursed a grudge against the household head because of his gaucheries of the previous night. The household head nursed a hangover, a guilty conscience, and a
tattooed foot. Sheila, Becky, and T. J. were equally out of
sorts, having endured for four weeks a camping father
turned professor and a camping mother increasingly un-

happy with the semicamping, semiprofessorial routine. Thus, the entire household sought solace and diversion at Burrell's Ford.

We found both—in abundance. Having set up camp, we were almost immediately adopted by Rex and Jerry, hospitable chaps who arrived five minutes after we did, unhitched their tent trailer, and extended a hand of friendship to everyone in the campground—which, at the moment, was us. Jerry had brought an enormous package of salt pork scraps, which he fried at high heat on their Coleman stove. Sitting in our lounge chairs across the loop road, we could hear it crackle. Shortly thereafter Rex sauntered into our site and invited us over. They had cooked way too much, he explained, and needed eating help.

It was a unique afternoon snack. Rex had been drinking I. W. Harper straight from the bottle, but he now produced glasses of the size a waiter sets before you when you order a small orange juice. Rex filled them to the brim, hand as steady as any waiter's. Jerry set the salt pork, swimming in two inches of grease, on the table, sat down opposite us, and urged us to dig in. We looked at the Ping-Pong-ball-sized curls of pork, at the formidably brimming juice glasses of I. W. Harper, then, finally, at the hospitable faces of Rex and Jerry—and dug in. Looks deceived! The snack was tasty and the bourbon cut the grease to an appetizing consistency. South Carolina "eat and drink" proved clearly superior to English "tea."

But our happy hour had only begun. While we dipped out the last of the side-meat curls, sucked our fingers, and sipped bourbon, Jerry fetched a guitar from the tent trailer. Picking a few introductory chords, he launched into the opening bars of Kris Kristofferson's "So Help Me, Jesus," then the number one hit sweeping the country.

"Precious Lord," he sang, "tell me what have I done, / To deserve even one . . . "

While we listened, he abruptly broke off. "Jesus!" he exclaimed. "What a song!" We waited for him to continue, but after strumming a few desultory, irrelevant chords, he set the guitar down and started scouring the empty skillet.

Whether or not Jerry knew all the song's lyrics is problematic. At least a dozen times in the next several days he picked up the guitar, strummed appropriate chords, and sang part of verse or chorus. Invariably, however, he would break off and call upon Jesus to witness to the greatness of the song, to the genius of Kris Kristofferson, or to the fact that had he, Jerry, written the song, he would never have to work another day in his life. Not once did he sing it through.

Jerry's talents as a guitarist were considerable, as a vocalist, passable. Rex Owen was a wonder on both counts. In the interims between Jerry's truncated Kristofferings, the two played duets. In addition to guitars they had a fiddle and a mandolin along. Rex played them all as the mood suited him. He also played spoons and the mouth harp. Indeed, he played mouth harp and mandolin simultaneously. We joined into rousing, ear-splitting singalongs. We sang "Beautiful Brown Eyes," "Sourwood Mountain," "The Fox and the Goose," "The Wreck on the Highway," "Power in the Blood," "The Tennessee Waltz," "The Kentucky Waltz," "The Wabash Cannonball," and a host of other folk, bluegrass, and country songs. They treated us to a rare version of "Dueling Banjos," featuring guitar and mandolin. In between, Jerry rendered fragments of Kristofferson.

Although we never inquired, we gathered from snatches of conversation that Rex and Jerry had taken unsanctioned vacation from both wives and work. Late that first evening Jerry underwent a change of heart and announced he was returning home. When Rex objected, Jerry swore at him, jumped in the Ford pickup, and roared out of the campground, wheels kicking gravel for twenty yards. Rex was unperturbed. "He don't mean nothing," he said. "It's just his way. He's only been married three months and this is his first real quarrel. And he didn't take his guitar. He'll be back."

Nor was Rex mistaken. When we sat down to breakfast next morning, he strolled over from the tent trailer. We invited him to join us, but he declined. So while we ate bacon, scrambled eggs, and hominy, he sat in a nearby lounge chair sipping his morning juice glass of I. W. Harper. Shortly after nine Jerry drove into the campground, parked the pickup, and began to clatter the skillet upon the stove. Rex, meanwhile, sat calmly, sipping his bourbon. "He'll be all right," he said. "But it don't pay to push a man."

Shortly thereafter we smelled salt pork crackling, then Jerry hollered "Breakfast!" Whereupon Rex got up out of the lounge chair. "He'll want you-all to come too," he said. "There'll be a plenty for everbody."

There was indeed plenty, although, like the feast of the previous afternoon, one-course fare. Having already eaten, we fingered a few curls. Jerry ate prodigiously, and even Rex abandoned his bourbon glass and devoured a plateful. Observing them, one could never have guessed that a quarrel had occurred. Indeed, whatever quarrels Rex and Jerry had with wives and work, we found them to be kindly, and quite generous with side meat and bourbon. They pampered the children outrageously, offering quarters for smiles, quarters for songs, quarters for thumbs, and quarters in apology for having no soda pop to offer.

In addition to his musical talents Rex was a magician of sorts. He entertained us with a series of tricks, none of them remarkably well done, but all rendered delightful by his chatter and good humor. When Sheila developed an earache the third day, he drove thirty miles over the mountains to purchase sweet oil to ease her pain. Of course he purchased two spare bottles of bourbon too, but that was an afterthought more or less.

When he brought the sweet oil to Sheila, he also brought the bourbon for sampling and evaluation. Indeed, his chief regret was that he had no moonshine to offer. "There's a lot of bad stuff made, for true," he told us. "But when it's done right, you get a sweet, pure taste this store-bought stuff can't match." Nevertheless, Rex Owen managed to make do with the store-bought stuff. He was indeed the drinkingest gentleman the household head has ever encountered. That peacemaker breakfast of salt pork was the only meal we ever saw him eat. But we never saw him without bottle, juice glass, or both in hand. Always he was grave and courtly, never loud or muddled. A puritan observing Rex would have seen a drunk. A sociologist might more objectively have labeled him an alcoholic. Northern city dwellers might have dismissed him as a hillbilly. To us he was Rex Owen, an amiable man who loved company and children, a talented artist who maintained, for sixteen hours every day, a harmoniously symbiotic relationship with a bottle.

Another artist, Ernest Hemingway, was once reproved by his father for having referred to real people in his short story, "The Doctor and the Doctor's Wife." Hemingway defended himself, saying it didn't matter because the people he named would never read his story anyway. That is probably true of the characters described above. People who pee in toilet corners are not usually voracious readers. One hardly expects an Alabama crossroads grocer or a retired factory worker to curl up with a good book. And since *Stressing and Unstressing* has no musical scores, I doubt that Rex Owen will notice it.

But I do not share Hemingway's cavalier sense of superiority. Hemingway's defense suggests a certain knowledge that Dick Boulton would have been angry had he chanced across his portrait in print. By contrast, I would welcome the country store man and Rex Owen to these pages. Reading, the metal detective might gain a sense of the apology owed him. And even the Texarkana trio might be led to consider the possibility that VD in the minds of others might stand for "violations of decorum."

But Hemingway was probably right. The people who people these pages will never read them. To us they were memorable because of their singular character and behavior. But the country store man undoubtedly played good samaritan to people who were not from Iowa; the metal detective doubtless encountered in later days campers both kinder and crueler than we. In short, because they, not we, made the encounters memorable, they might fail to recognize themselves, even were they to read these pages. Like the so-called lower creatures we encountered, part of their memorability stemmed from their lack of self-consciousness.

That is, the characters portrayed above and most of the lower creatures are unself-conscious. Badgers and snakes are another matter entirely.

Fearful
Fauna
of the
Forest

PREPARATORY TO EMBARKING on our first summer trip in 1967, we bought a snakebite kit. We were headed into the South—a region, we understood, noted for having state snakes in addition to traditional state birds and flowers. Assuming that there would be a water moccasin in every creek, a rattler sunning itself on every large rock, and a cottonmouth or copperhead lurking under every tangle of kudzu, we decided to enter the region forearmed. The kit cost $1.50 and was probably worth the price, given the sense of security it afforded us. That first summer we scrupulously carried it on every hike away from camp. Whether it would truly have served its purpose we never found out, since we saw no snakes that summer. And as the years passed we became accustomed to sharing the wilderness with walking, flying, crawling, and slithering creatures and quit carrying the kit. Eventually we either lost it or threw it away.

In fact snakes were infrequent on our list of creatures observed in the wild. Seldom did we see one save for fleeting glimpses of one slithering out of sight. Never did we see

107

one coiled, ready to strike. On the one occasion when we saw an angry snake, it had no opportunity to coil. At Table Rock Lake in April 1968 two-and-a-half-year-old T. J. found a nine-inch minisnake on the lakeshore rocks. He picked it up by the tail somehow and, accompanied by his older sisters, came clambering up the path to our campsite, excitedly shouting and gesticulating. The snake was not shouting, but it certainly was excited. And its gesticulations were ardent and pronounced. During the brief period while we struggled to get our voices back, we watched its attempts to communicate its rage and distress. It executed a hieroglyphic three, a two, a series of interspersed sixes and *j*'s, several commas, a question mark or two, and, finally, an ampersand. The household head scanned the hieroglyphics and informed his son that the snake wanted to be put down. The outdoor kitchen administrator elaborated: the snake wanted to be put down and thrown away simultaneously—and without any hesitation on anyone's part. Actually both parents' words differed slightly from what has been recorded here. In any event they managed to communicate, T. J. complied, and the snake, apparently relieved at finding itself no longer airborne, wriggled out of sight.

Camping in Stephens State Forest near Lucas, Iowa, we had a rarer, more interesting experience involving snakes. While on a midmorning hike, we chanced upon two snakes engaged in copulation. It was a fascinating performance—a graceful admixture of slithers and writhings that gave the term *serpentine* new and immediate meaning. But the scene was rendered more touching because the snakes were aware of our presence. They reacted quite humanly. On the one hand they were shy and embarrassed by our intrusion; but having progressed to a point of serious involvement, they were understandably unwilling to quit. In effect, they attempted to compromise—that is, to continue and to escape simultaneously. One searches in vain for words to describe the scene. It involved slithering, writhing, coiling, and a determined movement away from where we stood. Indeed, snakes are falsely maligned creatures. Essentially they are modest and reserved and would prefer, like those paragons among children, to be neither seen nor heard.

In this characteristic they are not unlike skunks, who are also undeservedly feared and detested. While we saw no snakes that first summer, we made extensive acquaintance with skunks—an acquaintanceship mutually amicable. A skunk's sole desire in life is to eat garbage. Indulged in that desire, it is invariably docile and benign. Our first meeting with a skunk occurred while we were camped at Loft Mountain, in Shenandoah National Park. We had spent the day hiking the White Oak Canyon trail, returning to camp quite late. By the time the outdoor kitchen head had our tuna and noodle casserole dinner on the picnic table, it was dusk. Everyone was hungry, including the resident skunk that joined us shortly after we sat down. It was a well-mannered skunk, content with the scraps that accumulated under the table. When we finished, we let it lick the plates. Thereafter it joined us for dinner each evening, occasionally bringing a guest.

A campground ranger related an even more fascinating anecdote illustrative of the skunk's companionable nature. At Loft Mountain the garbage cans were sunk in the ground. According to the ranger, several campground skunks had learned to lift the lids. They would crawl into the cans each night and gorge themselves. Then, unable to get out, they would curl up contentedly in the liner bags and wait for the collectors to lift them out in the morning, whereupon they would waddle sedately away.

In 1971, camped at Spectacle Lake, near Eagle River, Wisconsin, we deliberately left our brown paper bag of scraps and cans outside our tent door as an enticement to wildlife. We never got the snapshot we hoped for because we forgot to bring our flash attachment in from the car. But we did get a night's free entertainment. About midnight a mother skunk and three skunklets ventured into the site. We watched them by flashlight while they feasted. Afterwards the kits began to frolic with each other and with the empty food tins—indulging themselves in a rattling good time. Not until dawn did they give up their game and file out of the campsite.

Other animals proved less disposed to content themselves with leftovers. At White Pines campground, in North Carolina, the park ranger stopped by personally to warn us about pesky raccoons. Having noted that we carried a styrofoam cooler, he advised us to store it in the car at night. Although we ignored his advice, we tied the lift-off lid securely with clothesline and weighted it down with a large rock. Each morning of the five we stayed there, we found an additional set of claw marks on the lid. We were undoubtedly fortunate that the raccoon did not destroy the cooler altogether.

Our neighbors to the north were not as fortunate. On the second night a raccoon unlatched their Coleman cooler and sampled most of the contents. The reader will perhaps recall White Pines—scene of the great plastic dining canopy debacle, the campground where neighbors so abundantly supplied us with food and drink. On this occasion, seeing an opportunity to return a kindness, we invited our coon-cheated friends to dine with us. This they courteously declined to do, there being apparently some ritual of hospitality involved. Because they lived nearby, they viewed themselves as hosts responsible for entertaining us. So we compromised, agreeing to dine with them later if in the meantime they would join us at our site for a predinner beer while we fixed an early meal for our children. They produced a partially frozen inch-thick sirloin, laid it on the unlit grill to finish thawing, and walked with us back to our site. We chatted and drank a round; had a second round; fed the children; chatted and watched the campfire; agreed that a third round would be in everyone's best interest; chatted some more; and in the gathering dusk, watched a red fox lope out of the underbrush, grab the sirloin off the grill, and disappear into the woods. After giving brief and fruitless chase, our neighbor returned and invited the household head to accompany him on a drive to Brevard's grocery. Everyone dined late that night—except the fox.

On our summer trip in 1969 we camped the first three nights at Chippewa River, a campground in the Chequamegan National Forest. Wildlife abounded, probably because we were the only campers there. The evening we arrived we saw a deer on the camp loop. There were dozens of chipmunks, all so tame they would take peanuts from one's hand. Barred owls hooted each night. On the second evening our dinner was interrupted by a sudden cloudburst. Rain gusted in under the dining canopy, so we grabbed our plates and scuttled into the tent to finish eating. Thirty seconds later an enormous raccoon ambled into the site, bounded up on the table, and helped himself to the dinner rolls we had neglected to bring in. The household head rushed out to rescue the food but paused when it became evident that the raccoon was not overly frightened. It peered around disdainfully, bared its teeth and hissed. Then shoving a roll in its mouth and tucking two more under its chin, it climbed down from the table and sauntered along the path toward the bathrooms, glancing back occasionally to see if it was being closely pursued. It was not being closely pursued. The household head had no intention of tangling with a disgruntled raccoon over possession of a fistful of dinner rolls.

Eventually this raccoon became enshrined in the Hettrick high wall household's literary hall of fame, since it served as a model for the leading character in a bedtime epic that began the next evening. Inspired by the raccoon's antics, the blower-up of air mattresses spun a story about a greedy raccoon named Smorgasbord, whose inordinate fondness for noodles resulted in his getting himself stuck in a campground garbage can, from which he was rescued by the chance passing of a stranger named George Bear McCutcheon. The story was not purely original. A. A. Milne, Lewis Carroll, and Joel Chandler Harris would all have recognized an occasional plagiarism in the tale and in ensuing episodes. But the children were satisfied, so the saga became a nightly affair. A few days later we stopped for lunch at a roadside park en route to our next stop at Franklin Lake, near Eagle River. When Becky discovered a half-grown raccoon curled in the bottom of a fifty gallon oil-drum waste-can, the storyteller's stock soared. The story was true! Smorgasbord lived!

This incident supplied the household head with an idea as to how to keep the narrative going. As we encountered other wildlife on the trip, they were added to the saga's cast of characters. Socrates Squirrel and a hemlock addict named Percival Pierpont Porcupine appeared shortly thereafter. The deer on Chippewa River's loop road was converted into the White Stag, a pompous and pedantic oaf who spoke in polysyllables and drank copious quantities of scotch.

For the next four or five years the saga of Smorgasbord was a mandatory bedtime ritual. Fortunately the household head had the great good sense to insist from the first that the saga could never be related inside a house. Thus his wits were taxed only during the camping months. Despite this reprieve he proved to have insufficient wits to survive the taxation. The narrative became increasingly threadbare; and eventually the children matured, became literary critics, and lost interest. Or maybe it was the author's introduction of too many characters that spoiled the saga. At one point, straining for effect, he created a whole commune of bears—Busch Bavarian Bear, P. B. Ribbon, an old bear named Bud the Wiser, a fat clown named Falstaff, and an ex–ballet performer, Hamms, who could dance the cancan. One can occasionally substitute a joke for narrative, even if the joke is stale. But the Smorgasbord story was being replaced by jokes, or perhaps it would be more accurate to say that the story was becoming a joke. Or maybe Sheila, Becky, and T. J. felt that the storyteller had not produced enough bears in the wild to justify the inclusion of so many in the saga.

Indeed, we seldom saw bears in their natural habitat. We saw a great many in Yellowstone, of course, sitting

. . . the camper's relationship with wild
forest fauna can never be entirely casual. . . .
One can kick a provoked chipmunk in the
teeth, thus demonstrating who is boss. . . .
But what if one provokes a skunk
that is facing away?

along the roadside begging food from passing motorists. But somehow the bears in Yellowstone seemed more like bears in a zoo: the animals were real, but the setting made them appear artificial. Occasionally we drove to campground garbage dumps to observe bears lumbering around through a hillside of paper, cans, boxes, and furniture; but the experience was usually more depressing than exhilarating.

A bear munching contentedly on garbage appears to be a sluggish, bovine creature. A bear on the move is something else altogether. In June 1972 we camped for a week at Cade's Cove, in the Smokies. Bears abounded in the area and bounded through the area—bold, hungry, resourceful bears. Nightly the ranger presenting the program at the outdoor amphitheater warned assembled campers that bears were numerous, could be dangerous, and should not be petted or photographed close up. Nightly he gave a brief lecture entitled "What to Do If a Bear Comes into Your Campsite."

"If a bear comes into your campsite," he said, "the best thing to do is walk quickly to your car, get in, roll up the windows, and wait for the bear to leave. Do not blow your horn, as that may cause the bear to panic; and a panicked bear is always extremely dangerous."

Although the ranger gave good sound advice, it did not always produce good results because the bears also attended the evening lecture. Having attended often, they hid in the bushes, not bothering to take notes. Instead they observed which campers were taking serious notes and thus appeared likely to follow the ranger's advice. Then they followed those campers home, marking the campsite numbers. The next evening a bear would return to the marked site promptly at dinnertime. Seeing it approach, the obedient camper and his family would retreat to the car and, through their rolled-up windows, watch the bear devour their dinner.

One can understand why a frustrated camper, watching an uninvited bear munching his steak and potato salad, might disregard advice and lean on his car horn.

Horn-honking is, after all, a time-honored and traditional American mode of expressing emotion. Jubilation at someone else's wedding or over a sports victory is certain to be celebrated by a jam session of horn-honking. And like the nightly ritual of pig-whooeying at the Iowa State Fair campgrounds, honking is contagious and communal. An out-of-sorts couple driving home from a spiritless afternoon's shopping at the mall find themselves emotionally reinvigorated by the honking horns of a passing group of celebrating motorists. They add their Klaxon to the general din, then drive on home, perhaps later to make love for the first time in several weeks.

Conversely, horn-honking vies with finger-gesturing as a symbolic mode of expressing displeasure. A motorist in a hurry honks his horn to alert the driver ahead that the light has turned green. The motorist in front honks back to suggest what the first honker can do with his impatience. A third motorist honks to convey his derision of both. In seconds the intersection becomes orchestral, with everyone joining in, letting off steam.

Whether out of need for sexual intercourse, a need to let off steam, or a genuine concern for a marauding bear, Cade's Cove erupted one evening into a veritable symphony. It began on the far side of the campground, four or five city blocks away, so we thought little of it and continued with dinner. But the wave of honking moved closer, and soon we saw the bear. We could not tell whether it was a celebrating bear, a panicked bear, or a bear intent on getting through the campground while the light stayed green. But it was clearly a bear on the move, loping in our direction. Without hesitation we scurried to the Plymouth wagon and rolled up our windows, perfectly willing to let the bear finish our half-eaten dinner. While we watched, it bounded into the adjacent site, paused to snatch an egg salad sandwich off the picnic table, then continued across the road and out of sight. We did not honk our horn, having no desire to disclose our whereabouts to the bear.

A moving bear is a thing of beauty but not a joy forever unless one is safely out of its path. Our general impression, garnered from only two experiences, was that a rapidly moving bear is a nimble and agile creature, capable of avoiding most obstacles in its way—if it chooses. Unfortunately the choice is always up to the bear. The attentive reader will bear in mind the fact that the Hettrick high wall household had become a Hettrick high wall household due to the fact that an exuberant Labrador puppy had found the household's former Wenzel tent to be a factual obstacle in its path. If an excited dog could destroy a small tent, a moving bear could certainly demolish a large one. After our experience at Cade's Cove our desire to view bears close up diminished. Indeed, our foremost hope was that any bears we might encounter in the future would be nimble, agile, and possessed of twenty/twenty vision. In short, we hoped they would take note of our tent and avoid it as they moved around in the night. For bears, we subsequently discovered, do a lot of moving around in the night. Indeed, an encounter with moving bears prompted our abrupt departure from Flour Lake in 1978.

Located about thirty miles north of Grand Marais, in Minnesota's Arrowhead region, Flour Lake had been a favorite camping spot since we discovered it in 1971. On that first occasion we arrived at Flour Lake following two weeks of dismal rainy weather. On the day we arrived the sun was restored to the sky, and two weeks of rain- and bug-free camping followed. That is doubtless one reason why we found the campground attractive. But the campground was remarkable in other ways. It featured one of the finest sites we found in thirteen years of camping—a tree-enclosed knoll, 150 feet distant from the designated parking spot, which was itself located on a dead-end spur off the loop road. We had privacy, shade, and a marvelous view of the lake. As a precaution against bears we had to lug cooler and grub box down the slope to store in the car at night, then back uphill every morning. But that was an inconvenience far overshadowed by the site's other merits.

The lake itself was large enough to be interesting, small enough to be explored by amateur canoeists. Our first afternoon there we were treated to a full hour's entertainment from the lake. One of two fishermen in a motorboat unwittingly caught a seagull that dived to intercept an artificial lure in midcast. It missed, but the lure snagged its wing. A melee, fascinating to observe, followed. The fishermen wished to free the gull, and the gull wished devoutly to be freed. But the parties were unable to achieve harmoniously their separate but mutual desires. Reeling in a seagull is not easy, but the fishermen finally accomplished it—to encounter then the problem of removing the lure. After several unsuccessful attempts they managed to net the bird. This only aggravated the gull's fear and ferocity—which it expressed by screaming. A ring-billed gull's ordinary cry is brazen enough. The cry of a fearful, enraged gull makes even a loon's laugh seem mild. After one fisherman had been shat upon and the other bitten so severely as to draw blood, they finally gave up and cut the line, whereupon the gull swam sullenly away, lure securely enwinged, line spiderwebbing the water behind.

We saw no bears at Flour Lake in 1971, although we explored several trails hoping to sight one. Since this was the year prior to our Cade's Cove scare, we were still foolishly eager to meet a hiking bear. But we had no such luck, good or ill.

In June 1973 we returned to Flour Lake for a week's stay. We saw one bear, a nimble adolescent that scurried out of the ditch into the woods as we drove up the Gunflint Trail. But we saw no bears in the campground. Even had there been bears, we would probably not have seen them. Mosquitoes and black flies swarmed so numerously that a bear more than ten feet away would have been murkily obscure at best. We applied Off, Deep Woods Off, and Cutter's in increasing quantities. We rubbed ointment on hands and faces, sprayed our clothing, the picnic table, and the tent. We even bought cans of Yard Guard and sprayed the area.

Nothing worked. A mosquito, landing on one's hand, would jerk back, repelled. But before it could lift off, it would encounter several hundred other mosquitoes engaged either in landing or in lifting off. The entire group would subsequently become enraged and begin fighting—kicking, scratching, and biting at whatever was near. What was nearest was us.

Black flies were even worse. A black fly's bite does not hurt initially, but in forty-eight hours the itching becomes intolerable. By that time it does not matter, however, since the camper has meanwhile been driven temporarily insane by another, even more unsettling antic of the black fly. Black flies are incurable narcissists. Nothing so thoroughly pleases a black fly as to be able to hover in midair while gazing at its reflected image. Its favorite mirror is the human eye. But being nearsighted, the black fly practically has to crawl into the eye to get a clear reflection. Waving a hand to discourage black flies from congregating in front of the eye is futile. The household head still suffers chronic bursitis in both shoulders—the direct result of five days of black fly–shooing.

Blinking is even more dangerous because the blinker invariably traps flies inside the eyelid. Once having experienced the advantage of a front-row seat, they are thereafter reluctant to leave. After four days that June the Hettrick household members would have warmly welcomed a marauding bear. Running from a bear would have momentarily diverted our minds from the insects.

Late in the afternoon of the fifth day the sun shone temporarily and a breeze stirred. The black flies disappeared momentarily, whereupon, temporarily regaining our sanity, we struck the tent, loaded our gear, and drove south toward home. Throughout the night the adults traded turns at the wheel, thus allowing the other to scratch.

But if black flies were the initial marauders to drive us from Flour Lake, the bears did so later. In 1978, circumstances permitting only a two-week summer trip, we decided to spend it all at Flour Lake. This time we lasted four days.

When we arrived, shortly after lunchtime on Saturday, we found the campground crowded and our favorite site

occupied. Although disappointed, we were not unduly surprised, since the site was so attractive. So we pitched camp
nearby, hoping the current occupants would turn out to be
weekenders. And indeed, on Sunday there was a general
exodus. By the time we had our equipment relocated on
the tree-enclosed knoll, we found ourselves sole occupants
of the campground. We ate dinner with gusto that evening,
charmed by the silence, pleased with the prospect of five
days of solitude. Not long after dinner the bears moved in
and occupied the thirty-three vacant sites.

We never knew precisely how many bears there were,
since we were reluctant to walk the roads to take a census.
From our bastion on the knoll we watched them venture
into nearby sites and root for stray tidbits. Always there
were one or two visible, sauntering out of the woods or
along the loop road. Occasionally we would hear a garbage
dumpster lid bang in a remote part of the campground.
Indeed, before the night was over, we had cause to rejoice
that both campground dumpsters were remote. Judging
from the volume of clatter and bang, there were more
bears congregated around each than the total number in
the household head's Smorgasbord saga.

The outdoor kitchen administrator awoke first on
Monday and thus had the dubious privilege of being the
first to sight a bear. It was standing a stone's throw away at
the foot of the knoll, calmly surveying our Dodge wagon,
apparently waiting for someone to unload the grub box so
it could begin breakfast. The outdoor kitchen administrator, in a tone at once peremptory and profane, ordered the
bear to leave. Her shout aroused the other household members, but it did not rout the bear. Instead, it quit surveying
the Dodge and began surveying the shouter on the knoll.
The latter, unsettled by the bear's audacity, picked up a
stone, threw it in the bear's general direction, then seized a
stick and began beating a cooking pot. After a moment's
hesitation the bear ambled into the underbrush.

The incident increased our apprehension. Although
still unwilling to confess fear openly, both adults began to
hope that by nightfall the campground would have more

human occupants. Outwardly we agreed it would be wise to police the area thoroughly, eliminating all trace of food scraps. As an additional precaution we transferred the canned goods from our utility trailer into the Dodge. The trailer lid, formed of a single piece of molded plastic, looked sturdy enough, but we feared it might not withstand the prying claws of a bear intent on eating pork and beans from a can.

We had some reason to hope that the bears might not return. Since weekend campers had filled the dumpsters, Monday, we reasoned, would surely be garbage-pickup day. Thereafter, if every household member licked the platter clean, very little garbage would accumulate in the dumpster, and the bears might not be attracted into the campground. Perhaps, like the campers, the bears would be weekenders. The thought that we might not see bears for five days did not distress us.

Later that day, acting on the assumption that the stick-beaten cooking pot had been instrumental in driving the morning bear away, we worked collectively to fashion a super pan-rattling device. We raided the dumpsters for tin cans, washed them thoroughly in the lake to rid them of food odor, then strung them on clothesline, one end of which we tied to a nearby pine tree, while bringing the other into the tent. Should a bear come sniffing around, we hoped to rattle him off. Meanwhile we waited for the garbage men. About four-thirty, when we had almost given up hope, the truck arrived. We ate our dinner with hopeful gusto, policed the grounds, carried our garbage to the remotest dumpster, rattled the rattling device to make certain it still rattled—then retired into the tent.

All slept dreamlessly, untroubled by bear noises. Strolling down the knoll to retrieve foodstuffs from the Dodge Tuesday morning, the household head noticed that the trailer tongue had fallen off the jack. But since no one had heard bear noises during the night, he dismissed the matter as an accident. When we discovered evidence to the contrary—a mound of fresh dung in the weeds behind the trailer—it was evening, late for breaking camp.

We seriously considered breaking camp however. By this time we were openly agreed that having the campground to ourselves was a distinct liability. Unfortunately our guidebook provided no information regarding bear probability in nearby campgrounds, while a glance at the map dashed any hope of driving out of bear country in less than five hours. One last alternative remained—to break camp, drive to Grand Marais, and spend the night in a motel. But that seemed both cowardly and expensive. And while admittedly a coward, the household head had never learned how to be a spendthrift. His fear of spending money far exceeded his fear of bears. So he mandated a final night's stay at Flour Lake.

Actually, we told ourselves, our fears were probably groundless, since a normal bear would surely never attack unless it panicked or saw its offspring threatened. Furthermore, our rattling device might frighten it away. So we planned our evening carefully. At ten o'clock we made a family foray to the bathrooms, carrying the lantern and all available flashlights, thus advertising our presence and our platoonlike solidarity. Returned to the tent, we cautioned the children to "hold it till morning," rattled the device, and tried to sleep.

Two bears showed up about midnight. As before, they focused their attention on the utility trailer. Even though we had removed the food, apparently some residue of odor remained. Or perhaps these were simply fun-loving bears laboring under the mistaken impression that the trailer was an outdoor pinball machine. In any event, they began rocking the trailer, trying either to gain access or to measure its "tilt" resistance.

We first became aware of their presence when the trailer tongue banged down off the jack. Starting up, the outdoor kitchen head shouted and rattled the rattling device. A brief silence ensued, then the trailer banged again. Then both bears got into the rhythm. Thereafter it is doubtful that they even heard the rattling device, their own created din being so much louder. After a while we gave up on the rattling device and listened to them rock the trailer. None of us had trouble "holding it."

Their game ended dramatically and with dispatch. Following an intermittent series of bangs and clatters, there came a loud report—a kind of ground-level sonic boom. A moment later there was a different kind of commotion: one bear departed forestward, crashing through the mooseweed undergrowth; the other rushed up the knoll and through our campsite, tangling with a guy rope in passage and bringing our dining canopy clattering down. That was the last we heard of the pinball-playing bears that night— that summer, in fact. In the morning we packed and left.

Although we fully expected to find our trailer destroyed, it actually took half an hour to find the damage. A bear had poked a toenail through the molded plastic lid and apparently that had caused the thunderclap, although the noise seemed altogether disproportionate to the damage. Once we had patched the pinprick hole with duct tape, the trailer was as watertight as ever.

Our dining canopy was likewise undamaged. But even though our equipment was unharmed, we were no less determined to leave Flour Lake to the bears. Probably the bear had not seen the guy rope it plunged into. But since it had chosen to rush up the knoll and through the middle of our site, we wondered if it cared at all about obstacles in its path. Had the Sears umbrella been in its way, would the bear have dodged or demolished it? We did not know. What we did know was that we did not want, ever again, to be that close to a panicked bear.

Panic is the key factor of course. Mosquitoes and black flies are almost the only wild creatures that will attack unprovoked. Even the bumblebees were patient with us the day we inadvertently blocked the entrance to their nest.

We were weekending near Knoxville, Iowa, in a small county park which had neither designated tent sites nor parking spurs. One simply drove off the main road and parked near a table, setting up the tent on grass. On Saturday we drove to Knoxville for lunch stuff. Returning, we parked the Rambler wagon about thirty feet from the picnic table on the side opposite the tent. By the time the outdoor kitchen head had sandwiches made, a dozen or so bumblebees were flying aimlessly around. By the time we finished lunch, hundreds were whirling in the air between the Rambler and our table.

Furthermore, they were buzzing in a tone the household head recognized. As a farm lad he once located a bumblebee nest in a hayfield. Indeed, he located it with a horse-drawn mower, the moving sickle of which dislodged the nest from its location. The evicted bees, in turn, located the farm lad and lodged an angry complaint. It was a traumatic experience that left the ex-hay mower psychologically scarred for life. Even after twenty years he would surrender to uncontrollable spasms of terror if a passing fly chanced to buzz melodiously. Here were no passing flies, however, but bees—huge black and yellow bumblebees whose tone of buzz indicated they were on the verge of lodging a complaint.

Having had less experience with bumblebees, the outdoor kitchen administrator was not totally paralyzed with fear. After watching them for a minute or so, she observed that they swarmed most concentratedly near the Rambler. Perhaps, she suggested, the wagon was blocking the nest. Acting on this suggestion, the household head got a tentative grip on his terror, cautiously circled the area of circling bees, approached the Rambler from the farther side, slipped in, started the engine, and drove forward about twenty feet. As a result he missed the climax. As soon as the car moved forward, the bees stopped circling, queued up, and disappeared into the underground nest that had been blocked by the rear wheel. In less than three seconds the air was clear. Bumblebees did not bother us thereafter, and we returned the courtesy willingly, removing the Rambler and all equipment to the other side of the picnic table.

Whether the bumblebees were in a state of panic is debatable. Most certainly they were less panicked than was the household head. But their behavior nonetheless supports the panic thesis broached a few paragraphs ago: wild creatures are not normally violent or aggressive. A panicked bear might charge; a provoked skunk will spray; a threatened snake will strike. Mosquitoes and black flies are exceptions of course. A mosquito is not allowed to vote in tribal council until it has sucked human blood. But four-footed and crawling creatures of the wild much prefer to be left alone and are practically never dangerous unless panicked or provoked.

That is, all four-footed creatures except badgers. A badger will go to any length to pick a quarrel. At least that was our experience with the badger we encountered in Yellow River State Forest in northeast Iowa. We were on a sightseeing drive when we noticed the badger sunning himself on the road shoulder. Thinking he would make a good addition to our collection of forest creature snapshots—chipmunks, fox squirrels, porcupines, skunks, raccoons, and bears feeding in garbage dumps—we pulled the Plymouth wagon onto the opposite shoulder to avoid startling him. That proved to be an unnecessary precaution. By the time we had the wagon parked, the badger was already scuttling across the road toward it. When the household head got out of the Plymouth, camera in hand, the badger veered and scuttled directly toward him. Without hesitation the household head got back into the Plymouth and slammed the door, whereupon the badger veered again and, scuttling forward, slashed at the front tire. We laughed, then took note of the length of his claws. When he slashed at the tire a second and third time, we drove away without getting a picture, the household head being altogether reluctant to change a tire with a badger helping.

Perhaps the badger believed as did various American Indian tribes that a photograph would rob him of his soul. Perhaps he was simply an ingrained misanthrope. Most certainly he was a disgruntled badger, although as nearly as we knew, we had done nothing to provoke him.

And therein lies the problem which dictates that the

camper's relationship with wild forest fauna can never be entirely casual. The mores of a skunk, bear, or badger necessarily differ from the mores of humans. With smaller creatures the problem is manageable. One can kick a provoked chipmunk in the teeth, thus demonstrating who is boss. One can retreat from a coiling snake. And so long as one is face-to-face with an angry skunk, the danger is minimal. But what if one provokes a skunk that is facing away? And how to know precisely what violates his sense of propriety? Who knows what inadvertent word or gesture might be construed as threat or insult by a bear?

Though one can never be absolutely safe, certain precautionary measures can be taken. To the camper or hiker who unexpectedly happens upon a potentially dangerous wild creature, I can offer some worthwhile advice: keep cool; act natural; pretend not to be afraid. And furthermore, should you happen across two bears copulating on a forest trail, always ask permission if you desire to watch.

Exploring the BWCA for Only $8,000 a Month

"IF WE TAKE FOREST ROADS, it's bound to be shorter and more scenic," he said.

Household head and kitchen administrator sat opposite each other at a Fall Lake campground picnic table. In the background a clothesline on which were draped a tent, mattress pads, and sleeping bags suggested that their two-week canoe-packing stint in the Boundary Waters Wilderness had concluded on a rainy note.

"Besides," the household head continued, "we can save gas."

"Are we in trouble money-wise?" she asked.

"Not too bad. We've got almost a week's worth of main groceries and a little over $150 cash. That should last two weeks if we're careful. But I can't see spending money for gas if we don't need to."

"You can't see spending money for *any*thing you don't need to," the kitchen head corrected him.

Ignoring her jibe, the household head returned to his study of a Superior Forest map. Essentially he was trying to plot a back-road shortcut from Ely to Flour Lake, a

126

campground on the Gunflint Trail, 70 miles to the east.

Seventy miles as the crow flies, that is. Taking the Boundary Waters canoe route, the crow would have about 100 miles of paddle and portage. Following main roads— the only roads showing on an ordinary state map—the crow would face a 175-mile drive. Saddled with a Chevette pulling a utility trailer, we did not have the crow's freedom to choose from alternate modes of travel. Hence the household head's search for back-road connections that would shorten the distance.

It was not an easy task. Comprised almost exclusively of forest, water, and swamp, Minnesota's Arrowhead region does not lend itself to extensive road construction. The only major road is Highway 61, which runs northeast along Lake Superior's shore from Duluth to Canada. Although several gravel or black top spurs connected coastal cities with inland towns or lakes due north, no single road linked Ely and Grand Marais, the only two cities in the region with a population over five hundred.

Possessed of a magnifying glass and a highly detailed forest map scaled at three miles per inch, the household head managed to outline a modified northeast passage to Flour Lake. It was not a clearly defined shortcut, since the various roads kept perversely dipping south toward Lake Superior or doubling north in the direction of some forlorn Boundary Waters outpost. Nevertheless, highlighted on the map, the route angled generally, if not consistently, eastward.

Precisely how much of a shortcut he had achieved it was impossible to calculate. Though highly detailed, the forest map provided no mileage information. Past experience confirmed that roads in the Arrowhead region seldom go straight in any direction for more than a quarter of a mile without bumping into a lake or marsh. But we could estimate the mileage in retrospect, we decided, since we knew the Chevette averaged twenty-two miles per gallon. By filling the tank in Ely, then refilling at the Shell station two miles north of the Flour Lake turnoff, we could get a good estimate. Ultimately we were unable to make the calculation; the Chevette went most of the distance without using any gas at all, and we completed the last thirty-two miles of the trip in a different car.

The route being fairly complicated, the household head red-penciled the map, then attached a handwritten set of instructions:

1. From Fall Lake, 8 mi W on Fernberg Rd to Ely
2. From Ely, about 20 mi SE on Highway 1 to Forest Road 173
3. E on FR 173 about 13 mi, then right on FR 373, just past Jack Pine Creek bridge
4. SE on FR 373, about 4 mi to FR 173
5. E on FR 173, about 5 mi to intersection just beyond Sawbill Landing
6. Right on FR 175, about 8 mi E to County Road 7
7. NE on CR 7, about 14 mi to CR 3
8. E on CR 3, about 8 mi to CR 2 (the Sawbill Trail)
9. S on CR 2, ½ mi to FR 170
10. NE on FR 170, about 2 mi to FR 165
11. E on FR 165, about 30 mi to CR 27 (NOTE: Somewhere along the way FR 165 becomes FR 153)
12. S on CR 27, past Devil Track Lake, about 9 mi to FR 154
13. NE on FR 154, about 11 mi to CR 12 (the Gunflint)
14. NW on the Gunflint, about 15 mi to Flour Lake turnoff

Shown the map and the set of instructions, the outdoor kitchen head expressed misgivings that the route could be successfully navigated. "Sooner or later," she warned, "we're either going to get stuck, get lost, or run into a dead end."

"If a road doesn't look solid, we won't take it," the household head reassured her. "We can always unhitch the trailer and turn it around by hand if we get in a tight fix. And we've got all day to make the trip. If we get lost, no big deal; we can always backtrack. Having to drive a few extra miles isn't going to hurt us."

Out of all his reassurances, the last was pure prophecy.

We left Fall Lake about eight o'clock the next morning, negotiating the various twists and turns without incident.

Shortly after nine o'clock a burst of bird song prompted us to stop the Chevette and comb the roadside shrubbery with binoculars. Eventually we located the songster—a strikingly marked mourning warbler, the first we had seen in several years. Returning to the car, we had yet another of our senses activated: something smelled like burned rubber. We checked the tires and the hoses under the hood. Finding nothing wrong, we drove onward.

Landmark checkpoints passed with reassuring regularity: the South Kawishiwi River, Jack Pine Creek, Sylvania Lake, Sawbill Landing, Plum Lake, Dumbbell River, Wye Lake, Windy Lake. Shortly after ten o'clock we turned north on County Road 7, a winding road with a number of grades steep enough to force a shift into second gear. After one such shift the smell of burning rubber wafted unmistakably under our noses. Worried, we stopped the Chevette and examined tires and hoses. Still nothing.

But we were right to be worried. When we attempted to start up again, nothing happened. The engine ran, the clutch pedal depressed, and the shift lever moved freely. The Chevette itself refused to move.

Prospects were not encouraging. The nearest certain tow service was in Grand Marais, fifty to sixty miles distant. The closest probable telephone was at the Sawbill Outfitters, twelve to fifteen miles away—not an imposing distance if one could hitch a ride. The difficulty lay in finding a kindly motorist going in that direction. Indeed, the difficulty lay in finding a motorist, kind *or* cruel. Since turning onto the first forest road, we had not met, passed, or been passed by a single moving vehicle.

We had some cause for hope however. Pickups and Igloo food coolers lined the road a football field's distance, and we could hear logging machinery at work. Failing to hitch a ride before noon, we hoped to persuade a logger to sacrifice part of his lunch hour and drive us to a phone. Meanwhile we waited, slapped at mosquitoes, and scanned the underbrush with binoculars. Mourning warblers seemed ubiquitous.

Around eleven-thirty an empty logging truck appeared

on the road, coming from the east. Ideally the household head would have preferred a ride toward Grand Marais, but this being the first back-road vehicle he had seen all morning, he decided not to be choosy. So he stationed himself in the middle of the road and began waving his seed corn cap. He very quickly abandoned that station for the ditch, however, when it became apparent that the trucker had no intention of stopping. Indeed, the truck held steadily to the middle of the road, seemingly intent on bowling Chevette, canoe, and trailer into the ditch on top of the capless household head. At the last minute the truck veered slightly and roared past with inches to spare.

In one sense the driver of the eighteen-wheeler had no choice but to shave the Chevette closely, the road being quite narrow at that juncture. That he chose to squeeze past at fifty miles per hour was somewhat disconcerting however. If he wished to convey the impression that he was reluctant to stop for hitchhikers, his maneuver was generally successful.

No more vehicles passed that morning. Promptly at twelve o'clock the noise of the logging machinery subsided, and shortly thereafter four young men strolled out of the woods and settled down by their Igloo lunch boxes. Although impatient to obtain help, the household head appreciated the wisdom of the old adage: "Wait to ask your favor until a man's mouth is empty, his stomach full." Accordingly, he waited until one of the men rose, stretched, and lit a cigarette. Then he walked down the road. Since no one seemed particularly anxious to greet him, he took the initiative. Pulling out his wallet, he waved it and inquired, "Is it worth $20 to one of you to drive me to a phone? My car's broke down."

The loggers gave no indication that they were impressed by the waving wallet. Indeed, they gave no indication that they were moved by the wallet waver's predicament. Their case was stated by the youngest of the crew, the apparent foreman. "We just can't do it," he said. "We're working for my dad and this is the first dry day we've had in weeks." Then, noting the household head's expression of dismay, he added, "There'll be a logging truck come by in about an hour. He's loading our timber right now. He can give you a ride to the sawmill north of Grand Marais and you can phone for help from there."

Having already tried to flag down one logging truck, the household head was not overly enthusiastic about the prospect of hailing another. On the other hand, as the outdoor kitchen head succinctly noted, the idea of camping on the road forever was even less appealing. And it appeared that only loggers used the road.

Shortly after one o'clock the whine of a diesel engine became audible, and minutes later the truck labored over the brow of the hill a quarter mile distant. Surmising that the trucker would be unable to identify a wallet at that distance, the household head once more resorted to waving his cap, this time with more success. The driver began downshifting, eventually bringing the truck to a halt fifteen to twenty feet from the stranded Chevette.

Approaching, the household head pointed to his spouse, then to the Chevette, and outlined his problem: "We're lost!" he said. "I mean, we're stranded. Our clutch went out. The loggers back there told us you might give me a ride to Grand Marais."

Leaning out the cab window, the trucker gazed down silently. After a minute he unlatched the cab door and dismounted to the road. "Having a little trouble, eh?" he said.

"Our clutch burned out; we can't move," the household head explained.

"Can't move, eh?" The trucker, a lad in his midtwenties, walked to the Chevette, lay down, and skootched himself under the front bumper, head first. "Say it's the clutch, eh?" he said, gazing up into the engine.

"It smelled like burned rubber," the household head replied. "The motor runs, the car's in gear; but it won't move."

The trucker lay still for another minute. Then he inched himself out from under the Chevette. "I don't know anything at all about clutches on *these* things," he said, his tone implying absolute contempt for any vehicle with fewer than eighteen wheels or gears. He walked back to his truck. "I don't go to Grand Marais," he said. "I stay out of towns. The sawmill's north on the Gunflint. Know where that is?"

"That'll be fine," the household head assured him. "I can call a tow truck from there, can't I?"

Assured that the sawmill had a telephone, the household head assured the kitchen administrator that he would return with a tow truck as quickly as possible. Then, leaving her to guard car, canoe, and trailer, he climbed into the truck's cab, eager to begin the first lap of his journey in search of a tow.

It was a three-hour journey, mostly completed in silence. While the trucker was not in the least unfriendly, he tended to reticence. For the first half hour the household head managed to keep a dialogue going by asking questions, in the course of which he learned that the trucker lived with wife and children in Isabella, that the truck had thirty-two forward gears, that it was a new rig purchased earlier in the spring, that the lad was an independent hauler, that logging had been seriously curtailed by the rainy weather, and that the young trucker was more than a little bit worried about making payments.

"If I can make it through to winter, I should be all right," he said. "Once it freezes up you can get into the marshy areas and do some real hauling. Right now, these soft roads slow you up."

This last bit of information prompted the household head to observe that the trucker was indeed steering his rig down the dead center of the road. Just how prepared the driver was to maintain that position soon became evident.

After a half hour's traverse of a long level stretch the truck approached and crested a slight rise—so slight that the driver had not been forced to downshift. But it was a knoll of sufficient height to conceal what lay beyond. At the bottom, perhaps fifty yards distant, a deer stood in the road's center. Behind it, perhaps another twenty yards, a car sat, angled across the middle into the wrong lane. The driver had parked thus in order to photograph the deer without getting out of the car.

Although the logging truck's speed was only twenty-five or thirty miles per hour, things happened so quickly thereafter that the mere act of describing them sequentially misses the effect. The trucker neither braked nor let up on the accelerator. Reaching out the window, he squeezed off three quick blasts on his air horn and bore down on the assemblage below, meanwhile holding unswervingly to the road's center. The deer jerked its head around, froze momentarily, then disappeared in two quick bounds into the marsh. What the auto's driver was doing could not be so clearly ascertained. Both camera and cameraman disappeared from the window; there were some blurred, jerky movements behind the windshield; then the car itself jerked forward, whipped around, and careened ditchward, righting itself at the last minute. Somehow truck and car avoided collision. But looking down from the height of the passenger window, the household head got the distinct impression that the car had actually scuttled under the truck's bumper and out the side just ahead of the first set of dual wheels. He could see only a blue roof plus a frantically vibrating radio aerial, which had obviously experienced social contact with roadside shrubbery.

Once past the car the trucker glanced into his mirror, apparently to assure himself that it had neither crashed nor mired down in the soft roadside gravel. Satisfied that all was well, he initiated conversation for the first time that day. "God-damned tourists!" he said. "Driving these narrow back roads to look at the *scenery!* Stopping to look at a damn deer that's too damn dumb to get off the road. They shouldn't be allowed on these roads!"

The god-damned tourist in the truck's passenger seat wisely forebore reply. Indeed, he was busily engaged in a matter of motor control—trying to coax his large intestine into letting go its clutch on his esophagus. He was also entertaining the idea that he had seen but one logging truck that day, not two, that he was presently rolling down the road in company with the same person who had run him off the road four hours earlier. He decided he would not research that matter any further, either.

Apparently the Isabella trucker mistook the household head's silence for reproach, for he began vehemently to defend himself. "If people are going to drive these roads, they've got to get over," he insisted. "I can't afford to. If I run them off the road, I can pull them out. But if I get stuck, that's a whole day shot. Maybe two, if I have to unload." He looked at his cringing tourist-passenger. "You ever think of that?" he challenged.

"No," the household head muttered. In principle he agreed that those engaged in logging should have primary rights on logging roads. And since he had seen neither dead deer nor dead tourists along the roadside, he supposed that truckers made some effort to avoid running over them. He had no intention of putting his supposition to a test however.

The remainder of the journey was unmarked by incident. Shortly after four o'clock the Isabella trucker pulled his rig up outside the sawmill's main office. "There'll be a phone you can use in there," he said. "Good luck!"

"Thanks for helping us out." The household head offered a $20 bill, "Here's something for your trouble."

"Oh, no. I couldn't take that," the lad objected. But his tone betrayed him. Obviously he wanted to take it, probably had need of it, and clearly needed only a second urging.

The household head pressed the bill into the other's hand.

"Well, then, thanks," the trucker said. "I'll just wait here till you've got your tow lined up, eh?"

The household head thumbed the phone book's yellow pages, looked for an auto dealership, and called the first such listing, securing assurance that a tow truck would pick him up shortly.

Thanking the Isabella trucker once again, he turned down an offer to ride to the log pile and watch the unloading process. "I'd better wait here," he explained. "The tow truck should be here any minute now."

Forty minutes later the trucker was back, with his now-empty rig. "Still waiting, eh?" he said. "Well, they'll be along pretty soon. I'll tell your wife you're on your way."

Shortly thereafter CS Chev-Olds's white truck arrived. The sandy-haired driver leaned over, unlatched the passenger door, and held out his hand. "I'm Chuck," he said. "Where's your car?"

"It's stranded on County Road 7," the household head replied.

"Never heard of that road," Chuck said. "Is it on this side of the Divide?"

The household head's ulcer woke up and stretched as its keeper recalled that he had left the forest map in the Chevette. "I don't know where the Divide is," he said. "According to what the trucker I rode in with told me, we're about ten or fifteen miles west of where you turn onto the Old Marsh Lake Road."

"Never heard of that road either," Chuck said. "You must be across the Divide. I don't know that country at all."

"Do you have a map?" the household head asked. "Maybe I can show you. It's not too far past the Sawbill Landing," he added. "Just a mile or so past Windy Lake."

"Ten thousand lakes up here," Chuck shrugged. "You're stranded by one of them." He whistled tunelessly through his teeth. "Hoo boy, you must be *way* over there."

"It's fifty, sixty miles," the household head responded. "Took the logger over three hours to get here, loaded."

"Well, we'll just have to see," Chuck said. He shifted into gear and nosed the pickup out onto the highway. "Did you come from that way?" he asked, pointing left.

The household head nodded, and thus the return to the scene of the accident began, Chuck's gesture having set in motion the method by which the search for the stranded Chevette would be carried out. Arriving at an intersection, Chuck would slow or stop. "Did you turn here?" he would ask; or if the road dead-ended, "Which way now?" In the interim he whistled and sang bawdy snatches about his girl, Lulu.

At each crossroad the household head was able to indicate the correct backtrack with a fair degree of certainty. He would have been happier, however, had he caught sight of the Isabella trucker on the road ahead. After half an hour, during which Chuck maintained his fifty-mile-per-hour speed, the navigator-passenger began to feel nervous and uncertain.

"I sure hope we're still on the right road," he said.

"Oh, we'll find your car all right," Chuck assured him. "There ain't that many roads in this area. Got nothing to do tonight anyway. Never is much to do in Grand Marais, even on the weekend. Just drink a few beers and hump the old lady. What kinda car you got?"

"A 1978 Chevette," said the household head. Then as the pickup topped a rise, "That may be it up ahead."

It was indeed the stranded Chevette—within it the marooned outdoor kitchen head, whose lonely five-hour vigil was now ended. She informed the household head that not a single car had passed. "You sure know how to pick roads," she said. "I didn't see a single soul until the loggers quit work. Then about fifteen minutes ago the trucker stopped and said you were coming. Where in hell were you?" she complained. "How could the truck beat you back here?"

"If you were a deer or a tourist, you'd know," he said. "But it's too complicated to explain now."

The tow trip back to Grand Marais was slower and otherwise uneventful. Out of courtesy to his lady passenger Chuck abandoned his Lulu song, although he still kept up a steady stream of conversation. As he drove into the outskirts of the town, he turned and asked, "Know how you're going to spend the night?"

"Find a motel, I guess," the household head replied.

There's one across the street from our lot," said Chuck. "Good place, not expensive. Want me to take care of it for you?" He wheeled the tow truck into the motel lot—car, canoe, and trailer trailing, each in its ordered place. "You wait here," he said, bringing the assemblage to a halt. "I'll see what's what."

He strode into the motel. Emerging a few minutes later, he announced, "Everything's set. Here's your key. We'll get you settled in and you can register later.

"Don't you worry about your stuff," he continued, as he helped carry clothes, binoculars, and food cooler into the motel. "I'll lock your car and trailer inside the shop. Probably won't get around to looking at it right away in the morning though. You might as well sleep late. I've arranged with the folks in there"—he nodded toward the office—"to let you stay past checkout time if it's late getting word on your car.

"Lots of good places to eat here," he assured them, anticipating the question. "And they all put their prices in the window too. Good fish dinners tonight. No! Tonight's Thursday, isn't it? Anyway, just shop around. It's all good food.

"Tell you what though," Chuck was holding the truck door open now, preparatory to completing the last lap of the tow. "Do you people fish? Why don't you get up early, walk out on those rocks past the lighthouse, and get you some lake trout. Cousin of mine caught four nice ones Monday, using a . . . what was it now? Oh yeah, a rooster tail. Want to get your rods out of the car?"

Grateful as they were to Chuck for his good-natured concern for their well-being and pleasure, the household head and his wife were nevertheless tired and hungry— more interested in broiled than in breathing fish. Promising to stop by the shop for fishing rods in the morning, they dismissed their whistling benefactor. Shortly thereafter they sauntered forth to sample Grand Marais cuisine.

Over T-bones they discussed current financial prospects—all admittedly bleak. Subtracting the $20 given to the Isabella trucker, there remained less than $140 of unspent vacation money. A new or rebuilt clutch would probably cost that and more—not to mention the tow bill, the motel bill, the dinner bill . . .

"Can we put it on MasterCard?" the kitchen administrator asked.

"It'd put us right to the limit, maybe over. I'm afraid

this whole thing could cost five, six hundred dollars before we're through."

The kitchen head buttered a roll. "The car's not worth that, is it? If that rust hole on the floor gets any bigger, the foot feed's going to drop through one of these days."

The household head washed down a last bite of steak with a swallow of beer. "We don't have any choice but to fix it. We're still making payments on the damned thing."

The kitchen head lit a Parliament. "You've said often enough that you're tired of shoddy, used stuff that always quits working. Have you thought of buying a new car?"

The household head snorted. "Of *course* I have," he said. "But if we can't afford to trade for a used car, how the devil could we afford a new one? That doesn't make any sense at all."

"Well, I'm sure you'll figure something out," she soothed. "You ready to leave?"

That night the Devil that the household head had invoked over dinner appeared to him in a dream. Smelling like burned rubber, alternately roaring like a logging truck and whistling "Bang Bang Lulu" through his teeth, the Devil carried the terrified household head high up to the deck of a gigantic fire lookout tower. Below, an expanse of hillside had been clearcut by loggers. Acres of used and junk cars were scattered between bulldozed clumps of smoldering birch and pine branches. The Devil shifted to a lower gear, belched a gobbet of smoke, then spat out a mourning warbler. The latter perched on the household head's left wrist, then swelled to parrot size. When it spoke, however, its voice was unmistakably that which the outdoor kitchen head employed on those occasions when, from the passenger seat, she perceived that her husband needed advice in such matters as slowing down for curves or braking for stop signs.

"That doesn't make any sense at all!" the devilish parrot-passenger said. "Let them eat steak! Let them eat steak!"

Immediately the junked cars began sounding air horns. A camera on three aluminum legs stumbled out of a smashed Chevette, leaped a clump of burning brush, and disappeared over the crest of the hill beyond. And the household head awoke, aware that he had reached a crossroads in his life but that the choice of direction was not his to make. The next day's events had been foreshadowed and determined nineteen years before.

When the household head first began teaching at Drake, all faculty salaries were paid on the basis of nine-month contracts. Although technically the university's affiliation with the Disciples of Christ church had been discontinued, faculty were still expected to fast during the summer months. The only recourse to starvation was to teach full time through both summer terms—for which one received a monthly check slightly more than half that of those during regular term.

In the summer of 1965 the household head was assigned a single summer session. What this meant was, that after June 30 his wife and two daughters would want to continue to eat despite the fact that he would receive no more paychecks. And since he planned to ask the bank for a summer's moratorium on his car loan, he dared not ask for additional money from that source. In short, while it appeared that the household would barely be able to live through the summer, eating would be out of the question.

An afternoon's budgetary consultation convinced the household adults that disaster could be avoided only by adapting principles of Keynesian economics to fit the current crisis. Accordingly, the household head borrowed ten dollars from his mother-in-law, took it to a local meat market, and tendered it as a down payment on a half carcass of beef. "I'll pay you the rest at the end of September," he promised the manager. Perhaps because the meat market man was a Drake alumnus, he was prompted to be generous; perhaps he was simply less ruminant than the cows he butchered. In any case he agreed to supply a side of beef on those terms.

Although the general larder was scant that summer, there was always meat on the table. Meat was standard fare at every meal. Occasionally a leftover hamburger casserole served as side dish to a main course of grilled red meat. After that summer Sheila and Becky ate meat sparingly for several years. Even the adults wearied of such monotonously hearty fare. On one occasion, when four-year-old Sheila begged for a cookie, her exasperated mother replied, "We don't *have* any cookies! Go thaw out a steak."

Nevertheless the household head learned an important lesson that summer—a lesson Ben Franklin's Poor Richard might have summarized thus: Failing in all efforts to make both ends meet, buy meat with one of the ends. Now the Devil, disguised first as a mourning warbler, then a parrot, then as the outdoor kitchen administrator, had reminded him of this principle in a dream.

Accordingly, when Chris Nicholias, the CS Chev-Olds floor manager, informed him the next morning that clutch repair would cost $300, the household head took the news casually. Informed further that the Chevette could not be repaired before Monday, he was calm. "We can't wait around that long," he said. "What do you have in the way of new, four-cylinder cars?"

Chris Nicholias pointed to a dark blue Chevy Cavalier sitting in the showroom. "That's all we have," he said.

"All right," the household head replied. "What'll you give me on a trade?"

The sales manager hesitated. Indeed, it appeared that he feared he was being snookered into selling a new car. Finally he said, "Well, I'll have to look your car over to get an estimate."

"You do that," the household head rejoined. "I'll need an exact figure."

Throughout the day he sustained the tone of a busy executive who can't be bothered with trivial details. When the shop manager returned with an estimate, the household head accepted it without dickering. "Now add in the tow bill and the charges for installing a hitch and wiring it to pull the trailer," he ordered. "I want to take care of everything with one check."

Chris Nicholias was obviously uncomfortable with the

prospect of accepting an out-of-state personal check for
$6500. But since he made no overt objection, the house-
hold head let him suffer in silence.

Having finally discovered exactly how much of the
money he didn't have the Cavalier was going to cost him,
the household head phoned his local credit union long distance. "I'm in Grand Marais, Minnesota," he told the loan
officer at the other end of the line. "My car broke down and
I'm buying a new Chevy Cavalier. I'll be writing a check for
about $6500. I need you to cover that for me until I get
back from vacation in two weeks. I'll drop in then and sign
the papers. Okay? Oh! I'll need another $1500 to pay off
the old car loan too." He waited, fully expecting the other
to ask, "Have you gone completely mad?" Instead, the
loan officer assured him such a deal could be worked out.

"Thanks a lot." The household head started to hang
up but was restrained by Chris Nicholias. "I'd like to talk
to them too, if you don't mind," he said.

"Sure thing," the household head handed over the
phone. Chris began asking a few routine credit questions
while the would-be Cavalier owner cringed, waiting for the
moment when someone would shout, "Look! Look! The
emperor has no clothes."

But nothing happened. Once Chris had assured himself that there really was a genuine loan officer represent-
ing a bona fide credit union on the other end of the line, he
mellowed noticeably. When he hung up the phone, he actually smiled—for the first time since the household head
had offered to buy a car.

Chuck, the tow man, was more exuberant. "You just
came in here and bought a new car just like that, eh?" he
said. "Well, I'm damned, you sure could've fooled me. Here
I thought yesterday you were worried about money."

"Things change, I guess," the household head muttered.

"Well, we'll get you on your way soon as we can,"
Chuck said.

By midafternoon the Chevy was ready. With trailer
hitched behind and canoe secured atop, the rewheeled

tourists freewheeled up the Gunflint Trail toward Flour Lake. As they passed the sawmill, the kitchen head suddenly asked, "What in the world was wrong with you last night? You were twisting and turning and babbling to beat all thunder. I'll swear you were imitating a power saw or some such thing."

Well, at least I didn't squawk like a parrot, the household head started to say, but checked himself, recognizing that such a retort would require additional explanation. And not knowing whether his spouse would be flattered by the role she played in his dream, he deemed it wiser to be as noncommittal as possible.

"I must have been dreaming," he said.

"I think I still am," the outdoor kitchen administrator said. "I never thought you'd *ever* buy a new car. What made you decide to do it? What got into you?"

The household head made no direct reply. Muttering something under his breath about the Devil, he let the matter drop.

Inching Along Afoot

IN OUR EARLY CAMPING YEARS we did a great deal of family hiking. Primarily we hiked because the household head was an assistant professor earning an instructor's salary, and hiking was inexpensive—cheap, in fact. Indeed, after an initial purchase of boots, knapsack, and water canteen, the hiker's expenses are virtually ended. Without having to exercise restraint, a hiker with three small children could spend a day without spending money, there being no toll booths, ice cream wagons, or souvenir stands on trails.

But the household head was also an enthusiastic devotee of hiking. Secretly he envisioned himself a twentieth century Daniel Boone, exploring trackless wastes without benefit of axe-blaze or compass, leading his family into the pathless wilderness where, far from the madding crowd, no smoke from a neighboring chimney would pollute nature's solitude and serenity.

In actuality he had a terrible sense of direction. As a graduate student at the University of Wisconsin he regularly got lost or disoriented walking the eighteen blocks from his Vilas Avenue apartment to the campus. Therefore, he feared to venture off a well-marked trail alone, sensing that he might never again see smoke spiraling from the chimney of anyone connected with civilization. Thus he was a zealous advocate of family hiking.

The outdoor kitchen head was a more conservative hiker. Essentially she preferred short, well-marked trails— a hike around the camp loop, for instance, or an alternate route to the bathroom. Unlike Mohammed, she was content to ignore the mountain that refused to come to her. But recognizing her husband's enthusiasm for exploratory hiking, she feared that, left to follow his own bent, he might, like an unwitting Pied Piper, lead her children away never more to be seen. Therefore, she joined him in his pastime, exerting what persuasion she could to ensure that the outings would be either ranger-led or family hikes on unambiguous trails.

Accordingly, that first summer while we camped in Shenandoah National Park, we assembled each morning for the ranger-led nature walk. But these excursions were generally unsatisfactory, for the ranger normally set a pace that the children, aged two to six, were either unprepared or unwilling to maintain. For Sheila, Becky, and T. J. such hikes were uninstructive since they never got to hear the ranger discourse on local flora and fauna. The only discourse they heard was parental: "Come on, let's go!" "Stop dawdling!" "Come on, you've got to keep up!"

After a few days their enthusiasm for hiking waned. Indeed, they rebelled. Sheila stated their grievance succinctly. "Why do we have to go on a hike to get yelled at?" she grumbled. "Why don't you just yell at us in camp?"

Recognizing a certain validity to the complaint, the adults offered compromise. We would take no more ranger-led expeditions, we agreed; instead we would fashion our own hikes, walk at a comfortable pace, and thus not have to nag.

The pattern of our family hikes seldom varied. The children invariably started out like puppies, rushing up the trail, rushing back to show us something they had picked or picked up, then rushing ahead again, shouting at us to "come look!" Before we caught up, they would be off again, clattering and chattering, frightening birds, beasts, and shrubbery.

By the time we hiked two miles, they had covered six. Having viewed the trail three times over, they were bored and ready to turn back. If we insisted on hiking forward, they would lag behind, grumble, and call repeatedly for rest stops. When we turned back, the pattern varied: if truly tired, they lagged and grumbled the more; if not, they began to cavort and gallop again, covering the trail for the fourth, fifth, and sixth times.

Thus we seldom completed a hike in the early years. Unless our destination was a Forest Service fire lookout tower, we completed only a few hikes on circular trails. Then, when the children had galloped their customary six miles and clamored to turn back, we could outfox them. Indeed, we often took advantage of their galloping tendencies to hoist them on their own hiking petard. "How far do you think we've come?" an adult would craftily ask. "At least five miles," they would reply. "Well," we would rejoin, "the map says the circle is six miles; we'll get home quicker by going ahead." By the time the children belatedly realized they had been suckered, it really was too late to turn back. It was not too late for them to lag and grumble however.

But the children's perverse trail behavior had one beneficial consequence; it taught us the value of destinationless hiking. Beginning a hike with the express intention of getting to a cave, a fire lookout tower, or a waterfall, one tends to concentrate too markedly on the goal—to forget, as Woody Guthrie put it, that "it's the goin' not the gettin' there that counts." Although we frequently broke our promise and nagged, gradually we became accustomed to not "gettin' there" and began to pay more attention to the immediate scenery. Consequently our hikes became less patterned and more pleasurable.

Actually, fire lookout towers were guaranteed getting-there goals. Sheila, Becky, and T. J. never failed to complete a fire tower hike, an achievement the household head viewed with some ambivalence. On one hand, he admired their persistence and enthusiasm. But he also foresaw the unfolding drama. Having hiked determinedly to the tower, the children always wanted to climb it. Fearful of ladders, rendered nervous by open staircases and unwalled heights, the household head much preferred to admire fire towers from the ground.

But his preference carried little weight in the dialogue that invariably occurred at the foot of a climbable tower. "Let's climb up," they would urge. And he would reply, "No, not this time."

"Yes, this time," T. J. would insist.

"What's the point of hiking all the way *to* the tower if we're not going to climb it?" Becky would demand.

To the household head the whole point in hiking to a tower was precisely to turn around and hike home, leaving the tower unclimbed. But he instinctively recognized that the children would reject such reasoning.

So he tried to dissuade them using logic. "You don't want to climb up there," he urged.

"Yes we do," Sheila would insist. "Didn't we just say so?"

"But there's nothing to *see* up there," he would protest—an argument that invariably elicited a flurry of rebuttals.

"Maybe there *is*," T. J. would say.

"How do you know there's nothing to see if you haven't been up there?" Becky would argue.

And Sheila would plead, "Let's just go up and see if there's something to see."

Generally the household head gave in and accompanied the children on their fire tower climb. Essentially he viewed it as a trade-off: five minutes of heart-stopping, bowel-shuddering fear in exchange for peace and harmony on the return hike. Usually, a child allowed to climb a tower hikes homeward sturdily and contentedly; conversely, a child refused the pleasure of climbing a climb-

. . . he glanced at them
with growing suspicion. Were
they not as exhausted as he?
Was he the sole possessor of legs
that felt like concrete bridge supports?
Was he the only namby-pamby hiker in
the group? He was afraid to ask.

able tower is a surly, snot-nosed killjoy. The prospect of shepherding three snot-nosed malcontents homeward generally prejudiced the household head's decision.

It was a decision he always had to make alone. The outdoor kitchen head had a firm and principled aversion to climbing fire towers and a firm and principled contempt for anyone fool enough to climb one. If denying the children this treat spoiled their hike, so be it. If it spoiled their day, wrecked their vacation, and turned them into surly jerks for the rest of their lives, very well. *She* intended to stay on the ground.

Thus the task of accompanying the children on their fire tower climb always fell to the household head. Hitching up his belt, getting a firm grip on his bowels and an even tighter clutch on the handrail, he would make the agonizing ascent. Having reached the top, he always savagely reminded the children that he had been right—there was nothing to see. This was a bald-faced lie of course. There was much to see, were he but brave enough to open his eyes.

"Look how high we've come," Becky would shrill, gazing over the railing. That was the last thing the household head wanted to do. If forced to look, he wanted to look out—way, way out—and not way, way down to where the outdoor kitchen head lounged in contemptuous safety on the ground.

In truth, many lookout tower views were spectacular, could one have attained them without making the agonizing climb and the even more paralyzing descent. Not once, however, did we see a forest fire—which is, one assumes, what one is supposed to climb a tower to look for.

Primarily because we preferred to camp in national forests, we hiked to a great many fire lookout towers over the years. Generally the Forest Service located the tower on the highest peak, making it visible for miles. Just as invariably, the children spotted the tower and clamored to hike to it. Almost always there was a well-marked trail, and far too often the Forest Service designated the tower as safe for climbing.

Hiking to lookout towers offered some positive advantages however. Since the trail to the tower was always uphill, the return was generally pleasant. And having gotten to one's planned destination made arrival back at the trail head somehow more satisfying, even for veterans of destinationless hiking.

Hiking downhill toward one's destination is another matter. Hiking to a waterfall or abandoned flour mill, one tends to forget that the adage about "what goes up" is also binding when reversed. Except for saints and an occasional satellite, what goes up must eventually come down. There are no exceptions at all to the reverse rule: what hikes jauntily down a trail must climb laboriously back up. And the steeper the trail, the easier the descent and the greater the danger of going too far.

Such a fate befell the household head in the summer of 1970 when he hiked to the bottom of the Black Canyon of the Gunnison River. Although the entire hike supposedly covered only three miles, it involved a descent of 1300 feet. According to survey maps the return is also 1300 feet. The maps are wrong however. The Black Canyon of the Gunnison presents an optical illusion in that it appears to be symmetrical. In actuality it is five times as high, from bottom to top, as it is deep, from top to bottom.

The household head left the rim at eight-thirty in the morning and reached the bottom by ten o'clock. En route he learned that the word *precipitous* is not an abstraction. After half an hour he recuperated enough to sit and bend his knees without howling in agony. In another thirty minutes he was actually able to walk again. So, recognizing the need to keep his muscle spasms from knotting, he shuffled along the graveled bank of the Gunnison River, snapping pictures with his Polaroid. While he shuffled, he groaned; and while he groaned and shuffled, there flashed through his mind the answer to the riddle about the tree falling in the forest. If a lone hiker makes a knee-jarring descent into the Black Canyon of the Gunnison, then groans as he shuffles along the river bank, does anyone hear? No! Does anyone care? No! Such a shuffling, groaning hiker is as alone, as unheard, and as unloved as a tree that has fallen in the forest.

Solving the riddle did not improve his situation, however, since he still had the 6500-foot ascent ahead. He ate an early lunch, thus lightening the load in his day pack, filled his canteen from the sparkling waters of the Gunnison, and at eleven-thirty began his climb out of the canyon. By one o'clock his canteen was empty. This was not due to foolish overindulgence however. The conqueror of canyons, perceiving the need to lighten his load still further, had guzzled the water with that end in mind. He fleetingly entertained the notion of abandoning the empty canteen but decided its weight was negligible. An hour later he seriously entertained the notion of abandoning binoculars and camera, the only items in his day pack. Indeed, he would have done so, had he not been too exhausted to remove the day pack from his shoulders. By midafternoon he was seriously considering the notion of abandoning wife and children and living permanently on the canyon trail. Sometime after four o'clock he staggered out of the canyon and into the arms of the outdoor kitchen head, who held him up with one arm while, with the other, she proffered an opened can of Budweiser. The household head swallowed it whole; croaked for another, which he drank in three gulps; then, more casually sipping a third, looked levelly at his spouse and concocted the biggest lie of his life: "It really wasn't too bad, but I ran out of water about an hour ago."

Corollary to this experience the household head discovered a sequel to the tree-falling-in-the-forest riddle. If a lone hiker groans after he has staggered out of the Black Canyon of the Gunnison, no one hears, or hearing, feels that the groaner has earned anything other than his just desserts. Which is probably fair. The man who staggered into the outskirts of Newcastle, groaning under the weight of a knapsack stuffed with coal, probably wasn't much fussed over either.

Since he was the initiator of most hikes, the household

head always considered himself the rightful leader of such expeditions. Basically it was a hollow title, since no one else thought hikes needed a leader. But if they did not properly respect his role, as a rule they did not deride it either. And for the most part they loved him no less for his pretentiousness.

But it was a different matter altogether that July afternoon in 1970 when he led the household into Canyon de Chelly to view some twelfth-century cliff dwellings. By the time they straggled out of *that* canyon, his family had withdrawn their affection. That states the case rather too mildly. Sheila, Becky, and T. J. would doubtless have traded him for a different model father had the opportunity arisen. Indeed, they would have traded him for a cliff-dwelling Indian, eight hundred years dead and poorly preserved. Long before the hike was completed, they would certainly have sold him into slavery for a glass of water.

For the household head had led his family canteenless into the canyon under equatorial conditions. While personally supervising the filling of the canteen, he failed to supervise its transportation. Thus, when the party descended into the canyon, the canteen remained behind, sunning itself like a turtle on the hood of our Plymouth wagon.

No one noticed the oversight during the steep mile-and-a-half descent. But when the trail leveled for the last mile, everyone started calling for water. Everyone but the expedition's leader, that is. Having already noticed that the canteen was missing, he thought it prudent not to mention water.

Other household members were less prudent and more vocal. Becky loudly bemoaned the party's waterlessness, explicitly blaming the leader for his oversight. In response the leader committed a serious tactical blunder. Instead of hitting Becky alongside the head with a stick, thus discouraging reproach, he said that he was sorry. While he intended only commiseration, the other hikers chose to interpret his statement as an acknowledgement of guilt. Thus was the fetus of discord unwittingly conceived.

Arrived at the canyon's eastern wall, the household head inspected the ruins while the others searched for water. Finding none, they rejoined their leader, inspected the ruins, then unanimously agreed that the dwellings were similar to those they had examined at Mesa Verde two weeks before, in which case, they agreed further, the White House ruins had not been worth hiking to see, especially if one was dying of thirst. On this note of reproach the return journey began.

Since the first mile was level, the hikers' thirst ratio increased only in direct proportion to the axioms of distance and movement. That is, they became steadily thirstier and more reproachful with each step. At first the leader tried humor as a counter to reproach. At one point he remarked that the canteen, having sat on the Plymouth's hood for several hours now, would probably contain water useful only for cooking spaghetti. His witty sally fell on desiccated ears.

By the time they crossed the canyon floor and began the climb to the rim, the party's thirst ratio had reached raging proportions, rendering all but the household head bereft of reason and incapable of compassion. Although they no longer reproached their leader loudly, this was primarily because their throats were too parched to permit loud reproach. They compensated by muttering evil threats centering upon the advisability of slaying the leader on the spot and drinking his blood as a water substitute. Fearful for his life, the household head made one last attempt at self-justification. "I didn't forget the canteen all by myself," he argued hoarsely. "All five of us forgot it together."

"That's the last thing we'll ever do together," Sheila said.

"But there was only one quart," the leader protested. "That wouldn't have been enough to last."

"It would have lasted once around," T. J. said.

"I may be dumb enough to help forget the water," Becky added. "But I'm smart enough to know some water is better than none."

Thereafter, the party hiked in silence. But as the minutes progressed, the household head became increasingly aware that his children were ostracizing him. Sheila marched twenty yards in front; Becky and T. J. lagged behind a similar distance. Thus flanked fore and aft by three unyielding critics of his leadership, the household head trudged thirstily upward, pondering how he might redeem himself and regain their esteem.

Finally he hit upon a desperate measure. Where apology, humor, and logic failed, bribery might yet succeed. By dramatically demonstrating that for once he was not cheap, he would so surprise them that the walls of their hostility would crumble. Accordingly, he moistened his lips and launched his bribe. "When we get to the top," he croaked, "everybody can have all the strawberry pop they want."

There was no immediate response, but nobody threw rocks at him either, so the household head took heart. But later his heart misgave him as he remembered that strawberry pop for "everyone" would necessarily include himself, since the Coleman cooler in the Plymouth contained no beer and Canyon de Chelly was located in the middle of a Navajo reservation. Temporarily forgetting about the ban on firewater sales, the household head had, earlier that morning, asked for a case of beer at a crossroads grocery. The clerk's refusal was couched in tones that suggested that a leper had begged him for sun tan lotion. So the household head purchased a case of strawberry pop instead, not knowing whether the federal government or the Indians were responsible for the ban, but thinking the purchase might fittingly convey his red rage to either. Now, along with wife and children, he was going to have to put his mouth where his money went.

Drink strawberry pop he did, thus astonishing the other household members, who had countless times heard him declare he would much prefer liquid extract of horse to bottled soda pop. Of seventeen bottles consumed, the expedition's leader drank two. And the sight of their father drinking pop without even bothering to look around for a horse apparently softened the children's hearts. Or, perhaps they were impressed because he had actually honored his bribe. In any event their hostility diminished somewhat. Indeed, within a week domestic harmony was restored, and the household head was able once more to risk going out alone and unarmed in the presence of one or more of the children.

In this narrative's original draft the preceding paragraph differed from its present form. An additional sentence read: "And having thus so dramatically learned his lesson, the household head never again led his family, waterless, on a hike." But alas, even literary license has boundaries beyond which one cannot safely advance. Furthermore, Sheila, Becky, T. J., and the kitchen administrator will all doubtless read this narrative. Just the thought of their probable reaction to such an assertion has persuaded the author to keep the narrative more firmly affixed to truth. The truth is that a week later the household head led an expedition on a five-mile circle trail in Arches National Monument. Although the terrain was fairly level, the day was hot, so the hike lasted four hours. Becky and the outdoor kitchen head accompanied the leader on the hike. Sheila, T. J., and the canteen remained in camp.

Indeed, as the children grew older and more independent, family hikes became increasingly difficult to organize—primarily because only the blower-up of air mattresses had a genuine Everest complex. If a trail proved arduous and muscle-bruising, other household members willingly waved a white flag and turned back, thus posing a dilemma for their leader. He could push ahead alone, complete the hike, and finish the day feeling bone weary but superior; or, stifling his complex, he could turn back with the others, grouse at them for being spoilsports, and complete the day still feeling superior but without bone-weariness. Generally he chose the latter alternative because it offered the opportunity for unrestricted grousing.

One notable exception to this routine occurred in New

Hampshire in 1975. On that occasion the household head triumphed over white-flag namby-pambiness, leading a reduced party along a segment of the Appalachian Trail to the summit of Mt. Moosilauke. But the triumph was not undiluted.

The entire household left Wildwood Campground at eight forty-five and began the climb about nine—after first reading the trail head sign. The sign informed us that the summit was 3.2 miles distant, the trail difficult, hazardous in bad weather, and not recommended for amateurs or family hikers. Since we qualified on both counts, the outdoor kitchen head expressed doubts as to whether we should proceed. Her reservations were overridden by the blower-up of air mattresses. The Forest Service always exaggerated, he argued. Besides, the sign indicated that only the initial two miles were tough. Furthermore, it couldn't be too bad; hundreds of backpackers walked it every summer carrying forty-pound packs. Surely a family carrying only a day-pack lunch, binoculars, and two water canteens could match the accomplishment of pack-laden hikers.

Ultimately his bullying tactics prevailed, and shortly thereafter the blower-up of hiking possibilities led the way up the trail, accompanied by three unquestioning children and one dubious spouse.

It soon became apparent that the Forest Service had not exaggerated the trail's difficulty. All trails beginning from parking lots are deceptive, being at first broad, level, and gravel-strewn. This was a typical parking-lot trail for perhaps a hundred yards. Then it turned abruptly, narrowed, ascended sharply, and joined a mountain stream.

From that point on there was no recognizable trail—only nature-fashioned riprap alongside the stream's course. For three hours we struggled from boulder to boulder, grasping shrubbery branches for handholds, pausing every few minutes to pant and curse and allow the pain in our legs to subside. But the scenery was magnificent. Instead of flowing, the stream ricocheted off the mountain in a continuous series of cascades. All that morning we hiked beside it—often with spray in our faces.

Habitual birders, both adults carried uncased binoculars around their necks. These became increasingly a nuisance as the morning progressed, partly because of their weight but primarily because they threatened to dangle and bang to pieces against the rocks. Moreover, no birds were visible—a detail the household head several times plaintively remarked. His complaints provoked a response from Becky that summed up the trail with elegant accuracy. The birds, she explained tersely, were afraid of heights.

Lunchtime found us ascended to a flat rock slightly above a waterfall. And for the first time the water below the falls acted like a regular stream, flowing rather than cascading. "That means we've covered the two tough miles," the household head said confidently. "The rest should be pretty easy."

Other party members were less confident. T. J. joined the kitchen head in voting for a lunch break followed by return to the car. But the expedition's leader was stubbornly determined to continue. Angry because the Forest Service had accurately warned of the trail's difficulty, he was even angrier because the trail head sign had implied that he was a namby-pamby amateur hiker. His knowledge that he *was* a namby-pamby amateur only increased his rage.

So after lunch an agreement was struck. T. J. and the outdoor kitchen head elected to turn back, spend the afternoon in camp, then return to the trailhead at five. Sheila and Becky decided to accompany their father to the summit. Perhaps they were enjoying the hike, perhaps demonstrating loyalty; possibly they wanted to prove themselves superior to the birds that feared to venture so high. In any event the household head welcomed their company, unaware that he was acquiring witnesses to his later humiliation.

For another hour the trio lurched and toiled upward over rocks, following which the household head's confident lunchtime prophecy seemed vindicated. The trail veered away from the stream, gradually lost its rock-quarry aspect, broadened, and became walkable, albeit still steep. While halted for a breather, the expedition's leader heartily assured his daughters that they had now conquered the two difficult miles. The rest would be easy, he cheerfully asserted. This newest prophecy elicited no immediate response, Sheila and Becky being otherwise occupied in sharing the canteen's contents. More specifically, they were parceling out the dregs in the canteen, which had not been filled at lunchtime.

In a sense it was a natural oversight. Since we knew that the trail's beginning sector paralleled the stream, we had not bothered to fill the canteens at the campground. Once on the trail we drank directly from the stream. Thus the canteen contained only a few tablespoonsful of tepid water left over from some previous hike.

Observing the empty canteen, the household head for the first time contemplated the probable failure of the Moosilauke expedition. The grueling climb following the muscle-knotting lunch break had left him with legs that felt like bridge pillars with varicose veins. Undoubtedly his daughters felt worse and should therefore be spared the agony of going further. But the expedition's leader hated to admit defeat, his Everest complex having by now grown into a raging monomania. If necessary, he vowed to triumph over this trail alone or perish in the attempt. Yet deep in his consciousness, like a sulphur match aching to be struck, lay the knowledge that he wished neither to perish nor to triumph alone.

Accordingly, he proposed to Sheila and Becky that they continue up the trail with the canteen unfilled. In all likelihood, he argued, they would soon rejoin the stream or cross a tributary. They readily agreed—so readily, in fact, that he glanced at them with growing suspicion. Were they not as exhausted as he? Was he the sole possessor of legs that felt like concrete bridge supports? Was he the only namby-pamby hiker in the group? He was afraid to ask.

The hike resumed with the challenger of mountains plodding along on concrete legs while Sheila and Becky sauntered behind on apparently more supple ones. Although numerous switchbacks attested to the trail's continuing difficulty, the hikers made increasingly better progress. They also, as time passed, made the discovery that the trail had permanently departed from the stream, a fact which activated the children's latent Schlitzophrenia.

Since the next two hiking hours were uneventful, an explanation of this malady might appropriately fill a gap in the narrative. Prior to the midseventies Sunday beer sales were prohibited in Iowa. All taverns closed, and restaurants choosing to remain open stocked up on milk and iced tea. Supermarkets posted No Trespassing signs along the beer aisle.

Picture now a typical Iowa beer drinker—Horace Finkledunk. It is mid-September. Driving home Tuesday evening, Horace remembers his beer supply is low, so he purchases a twelve-pack. Actually, he has four beers in the fridge, a circumstance that ultimately leads to his disaster. Tuesday being an uphill weekday, Horace drinks two beers before dinner. Afterward he and Hortense watch TV. When she pops corn to make the ten o'clock news digestible, he eats his share and washes it down with a beer.

Wednesday is bowling night, so Horace drinks several beers before dinner, hoping to relax and break 200. When his high score of 142 displeases his teammates, he does not join them for pizza. After driving morosely home, he pops a frozen pizza into the oven. While it heats, he drinks a beer; while he eats it, another.

Thursday is baseball night on TV. An ardent Cardinal fan, Horace drinks no beer before dinner but cracks a can with the opening pitch. It is an exciting game, won by the Cards, five to four in the eleventh. Avidly cheering the relief pitcher on, Horace fails to notice that his fifth and last beer is a different brand.

On Friday Horace stops at a neighborhood tavern with some office buddies. They drink a round of martinis, then several more rounds, and when Horace arrives home well past dinnertime, he is plastered. Although he expects Hortense to raise hell, she greets him without comment, even when he knocks over a potted Swedish ivy plant while shrugging out of his jacket. She quietly warms up dinner, then sits across the table smoking a cigarette while he eats. Later, when he has untied a shoelace into an unsolvable knot, she untangles it, then when he passes out on the couch, covers him with a blanket. At eleven she wakes him for bed.

Hortense's generous behavior contributes directly to Horace's eventual Schlitzophrenia. A typical wife, she would ordinarily have been angrier than a cat in the vet's waiting room. But today she has been visited by her brother-in-law, Harold—a real creep who sat around bitching about her twin sister, Henrietta, then tried to borrow $200, meanwhile cadging two beers. Thoroughly disgusted with Harold, Hortense appreciates even a drunken Horace. Not a beer drinker herself, it does not occur to her that Horace would want to know about the diminished supply.

Horace wakes up Saturday, hung over and feeling guilty. Remembering his wife's forbearance the previous evening, he determines to be worthy of her good nature. Over breakfast he proposes a day of pleasure—the university football game that afternoon, dinner at a fancy restaurant, then a movie. The plan pleases Hortense, so they follow it. The Hawkeyes win, the steaks are grilled to perfection, the movie relaxes. By the time they arrive home, they are mellow, in the mood, and already suggestively exploring each other's physical geography. Intent on Central America, Horace forgets to check the refrigerator.

On Sunday Horace awakes and, still soaring on the updraft of yesterday's euphoria, offers to make breakfast. He struts downstairs, opens the fridge, and pokes around for the bacon, locating instead the single remaining beer. Immediately his euphoria evaporates. The prospect of nursing one beer through an afternoon of pro football fills him with dismay. Moreover, there is no bacon in the fridge.

Resigned, he drives to the supermarket and strides to the meat counter, located directly across the aisle from the beverages. Dropping the bacon in his cart, he eyes the six-packs of Pabst, Old Style, and Bud—all glistening with sweat beads of chill and lying attractively under a sign announcing No Sunday Beer Sales. Sadly Horace brings home the bacon and cooks breakfast, burning the toast and breaking two egg yolks. Since his two closest beer-drinking friends are out of town, there seems no possibility of sending out a Sunday SOS. All that long day Horace suffers the tortures of Schlitzophrenia.

Like Horace the Mt. Moosilauke hikers were un-bothered by thirst until it became apparent that the trail had permanently departed from the stream. Thereafter, Sheila and Becky loudly bemoaned the lack of water. But the household head did not much care. His elation at hav-ing triumphed over the trail rendered all other consider-ations trivial. When the party passed the sign indicating that the meadow they were entering was indeed the sum-mit, he turned to his daughters and exulted, "There, by god! That'll show 'em."

"Show who?" Sheila asked. "Mother and T. J.?"

"Let's look for water," Becky added.

Their casual attitude reawakened the Moosilauke con-queror's suspicion that his daughters had not found the trail to be as arduous as he had, so he momentarily stifled his jubilation. Looking around, he noted two backpackers reclining against a boulder at the far end of the meadow, where—so he assumed—they were resting after having reached the summit from the opposite direction. Ap-proaching, he inquired if they knew of a water source nearby. Yes, the lady replied, there was a spring two or three hundred feet off to the right. Sheila and Becky imme-diately trudged off to fill the canteen. The household head remained behind, exchanging introductions with Glen, an Ohio State University professor of economics, and his wife, Betty. Both appeared to be in their late fifties.

The household head took note of the couple's sun-browned faces and bulky packs. "You folks look like you've been on the trail a while," he said.

"Just about six weeks now," Glen replied. "We left Mt.

Katahdin in mid-June. With luck, we'll get to Springer Mountain sometime in October. But time doesn't matter if the weather holds," he added. "I'm on sabbatical."

"We'll never get to Georgia if you keep stopping for every trout stream," Betty said.

Glen smiled. "I found some good fishing in Maine," he explained. "Dawdled for two weeks and put us way behind schedule."

"How many miles do you cover in a day?" the household head asked.

"Anywhere from ten to twenty. Depends a lot on the trail," Glen said. "Right now we're making good time because we've eaten most of our trail food. Only three more days of macaroni." He smiled at Betty, then addressed the household head, "We restock in Hanover."

Now for years the household head had talked longingly and loudly of his desire to hike the Appalachian Trail in its entirety. He talked longingly out of genuine longing and loudly because he was certain that circumstances would never permit his being put to the test. Having hiked segments of the trail in Virginia and North Carolina, he had a healthy respect for its ruggedness. Nevertheless, he continued to pore over maps and bore his friends with his one-of-these-summers-I'm-going-to monologue, confident that, if never required to put his money where his mouth was, he would never end up with his foot in his mouth.

Indeed, had he paid attention to the word "Hanover," then pictured one of his pored-over maps, he would have avoided the taste of shoe leather this time as well. But he was flushed with the success of having mastered the three-mile Moosilauke climb. Even though it had taken six hours, he had demonstrated to the world that he was not a namby-pamby amateur. If the world was indifferent to his accomplishment, that was the world's loss. Besides, he had a captive Glen-and-Betty world in front of him.

Therefore assuming the tone of a modest but veteran backpacker, he agreed that fifteen miles would be a good day's hike if one were traveling light. While making this observation, he casually hefted Glen's pack—rather, his initial gesture was casual. The trail-foodless pack appeared to weigh something in excess of two hundred pounds.

Glen noticed his wince and smiled apologetically. "I guess it *is* a bit heavy," he said. "Betty and I don't pretend to be rugged souls. We like to be comfortable. There's a lot of luxury stuff in there: canned peanuts, extra camera equipment, my waders, stuff like that. We may never get to Georgia, but we'll enjoy ourselves.

"In fact," he continued, "I slowed us up again today, dawdling along with my camera. Took two rolls of film."

Seeing an opportunity to do the couple a favor while simultaneously making modest reference to his party's accomplishment, the household head interrupted, "Keep your camera handy on the way down. The first mile is pretty ordinary, but after that there're some spectacular cascades. It's a hell of a climb, but it shouldn't be too bad going down."

"We came that way today, too," Glen said. "I've never seen anything to match it. I sure hope the pictures turn out all right."

"You hiked up the trail ahead of us?" The stunned household head looked at Betty, at Glen, then at the bulky packs.

"We probably started an hour or so before you did," Glen said. "I got up here about fifteen minutes ago. Betty got tired of my dawdling and hiked ahead. She's been up here a couple of hours."

Meanwhile Sheila and Becky had returned with the filled canteen. They stood and looked questioningly at their father, who stood looking dumbfoundedly at the suntanned backpackers from Ohio.

"We never saw you on the trail," he accused.

"We left the campground a little after eight," said Glen. "Probably got to the trailhead about nine."

"About nine," the head of the namby-pambies mumbled.

"We camped next to you at Wildwood," Glen added. "Noticed your equipment. You've got some nice backpacking tents."

"We started up the trail at nine, too," Becky observed. "But Dad didn't stop to take pictures."

The Moosilauke conqueror glared at his daughter, debating whether to slay her outright or just deny her food and drink for the rest of the trip.

"Usually we camp on the trail," Glen said. "But we wanted to see Wildwood and figured the four-mile detour wouldn't make that much difference." He pushed himself up from the rock. "Well, Betty," he said, slinging his two-hundred-pound pack onto his shoulders, "you've been up here half the afternoon, and we've dawdled long enough. Best be on our way."

"Yes! For God's sake don't dawdle," the household head muttered. "Or you'll never get to Hanover by dinnertime." He muttered this to himself however. Aloud, he said only, "Good luck on the trail." Everyone shook hands; then the Ohio couple departed, innocently unaware that with each step they were trampling an ego into the Moosilauke meadow.

For the Iowa household the late afternoon descent was quiet and uneventful, swifter and easier than the climb. Approaching the flat rock above the waterfall, they discovered T. J. and the open air kitchen head waiting.

"You forgot to give me the car keys," the latter explained. "So we figured it would be more pleasant to wait here."

"He forgot to fill the canteen, too," Sheila said. "We had to hike all the way up without water. But we met some nice people at the top who showed us where a spring was."

"He had a camera and took a lot of pictures," Becky added. "His wife didn't wait for him."

"Never mind about that," the household head said. "We don't need to go into that at all." Then, discouraging further conversation, down the trail he led his troop, wearily placing, one before the other, his leaden feet of clay.

Out
of
Izaak
Walton's
League

OVER THE YEARS hiking was probably our least expensive recreational pastime. Fishing was another matter however. Although we kept no exact record of expenditures for rods, reels, tackle, lures, bait, licenses, and boat and canoe rental, we spent, as nearly as we can estimate, about thirty hours and twenty-five dollars for each fish we caught. We did not keep an exact record of our catches either; indeed, we had no reason to. Since we caught so few keepers, keeping track posed no difficulty. The species of fish, its size, the stream or lake from which we pulled it, the unusual circumstances attendant upon its being netted—all these details were indelibly stamped on our memory.

A regular reader of *Field and Stream* might jump to the hasty conclusion that we were poor fishermen. Such a reader would be inaccurate only in choice of adjective. We were not *poor* fishermen; we were utterly and hopelessly inept. Part of our failure stemmed from our penchant for comfort and convenience. Like the drunk who lost a quarter in the middle of the block but looked for it at the corner where the light was better, we tended to fish on our terms.

If both the fish and the mosquitoes were biting, we stayed in camp. Recognizing the preeminence of the sun, we always let it rise before we did. Never did we reward an early fish with a worm. Indeed, we seldom used worms, artificial lures being easier to attach and cast.

Over a decade of sporadic fishing we had minor success, netting, altogether, 24½ keepers. Admittedly an unimpressive total. Nevertheless, as the summary below conclusively demonstrates, each household member had his or her day on the pond.

TJ:	6 rainbow trout	6
BJ:	1 rainbow trout	1
SK:	4 rainbow trout	4
OKH:	1 rainbow trout, 1 catfish, 3 largemouth bass	5
HOH:	3 rainbow trout, 3 brook trout, 1 northern pike, 1 largemouth bass, ½ chinook salmon	8½
	Total	24½

Most of the rainbow trout were netted in the summer of 1977 during our sojourn at Seedhouse, a national forest campground on Colorado's western slope. That summer Seedhouse was the appointed rendezvous spot for members of the Great Drake Backpackers Association. The household head planned to temporarily abandon his family at Seedhouse while joining three professorial colleagues on a backpacking expedition to Three Island Lake, a primitive area in the Mt. Zirkel Wilderness. The three colleagues were a preacher of economics, leader of the expedition and preparer of victuals; a history professor, chief firebuilder and recorder of expenses; and a butterfly fanatic, whose role it was to supervise dishwashing and keep the campsite free from butterflies. The household head was the self-designated fisherman for the excursion.

There were only two islands and no fish at all in Three Island Lake. Fortunately the economics preacher had exercised forethought in packing supplies, so the expedition members ate heartily despite the designated fisherman's failure. In the meantime the failed fisherman's children were casually pulling trout out of a small tributary of the

Elk River, about a half mile from Seedhouse Campground.

Actually, the household head discovered the stream his children fished so successfully. Indeed, he caught two trout there on the day before he went backpacking, having located a spot where a large, flat rock jutted into the swift current, creating a trout hole one could fish without wading. Having gone three years without a keeper—his last being the half-salmon he netted in 1974—the household head was understandably elated. But he was even more excited with the prospect of fishing the wilderness area, where, he assumed, trout would be less fished for, thus more plentiful. How wrong he was has already been related. But his consternation at catching no trout at Three Island Lake was as nothing compared with his consternation when he returned from the expedition and heard the tales of Sheila's, Becky's, and T. J.'s fishing exploits.

Apparently they could have caught limitless numbers of trout had they dedicated themselves to the task. On the morning their father departed, Sheila and T. J. walked to the flat rock and returned within an hour, T. J. having caught two trout, Sheila one. Spurred to action by their easy success, Becky grabbed a rod and went a-fishing also. In half an hour she was back with a trout still dangling from the hook. Catching the fish had been child's play— which was fortunate, Becky being still a child. But she had not anticipated having to handle it. That proved difficult— impossible, in fact. Matters grew even more complicated when she discovered that her mother expected her to eat the trout she had caught. Firmly convinced that eating anything other than a frozen, packaged fish would be the equivalent of butchering and devouring a pet, Becky quit fishing altogether.

T. J. and Sheila were neither as squeamish nor as tenderhearted. Each subsequent morning T. J. marched to the trout hole and caught one fish—usually in the first five or ten minutes, once on his first cast. Having procured breakfast, he returned to camp, where a further ritual was enacted. First the outdoor kitchen administrator was required to snap a picture of T. J. and his trout; afterward he ate it, then quit fishing for the day, one trout meal being sufficient. Sheila had similar success on two of four mornings. Thus, while the less-than-complete angler spent four days dissolving salmon eggs and untangling his line, his children caught ten trout while fishing collectively two or three hours. Had they fished as persistently as did their father, they could have filled the fifty-four-quart Coleman cooler with trout.

They could have, that is, if the fish stories they told were true. The children insisted that they caught ten trout in the manner described above, and their mother corroborated their story. Furthermore, there were nine polaroid snapshots that seemed concretely to validate their claims: one picture of Becky holding a rod from which a trout still dangled, three separate shots of Sheila holding a trout, four shots of T. J. flaunting a fish, and one in which he grins above a heavy breakfast of two rainbows.

But it was precisely the pictures that instilled in the household head's mind the dark suspicion that he was being hoodwinked. In each photo the trout looked the same, while only the figure of the child changed. What if Sheila had been photographed holding T. J.'s fish? In that case perhaps only seven trout had been netted. On the other hand, if T. J. had borrowed Sheila's trout to pose for his single-catch photos, then perhaps the children had collectively caught only six fish—that is, Sheila's three, T. J.'s two, and Becky's still-on-the-line single trout.

It was a fascinating scenario, and the blower-up of air mattresses pursued it to its logical end. Ultimately he convened family members around the picnic table, announced that he had unraveled the mystery of the great rainbow trout bonanza, and charged them with collective fraud. There was, he conceded, concrete evidence that two trout had been caught—presumably by T. J. For the rest, he was convinced that Becky had taken one fish and attached it to a hook, while Sheila and T. J. passed the other back and forth, pausing between pictures to change clothes and rearrange the backdrop scenery. His accusation elicited both denial and ridicule. And since the trout—of whatever number—had been cleaned and eaten, there remained only the photographs as mute evidence ambiguously supporting both theories. So the household head reluctantly accepted the version which, no less reluctantly, he has recorded here. But like Richard Nixon he wishes to make one thing "crystal clear": if the children's story *is* true, it isn't fair.

Honesty compels the household head to admit, however, that this was not the only occasion when he was outfished by one or more family members. In 1974 at Neys, a campground in Ontario, he fished Lake Superior nine successive days without getting even a strike. Two factors accounted for his dogged persistence: the beauty of the fishing spot and the success of other household members.

Neys was located on Lake Superior's north shore close to a peninsula shaped like a crooked forefinger. At the extreme end of the peninsula a fingernail—an enormous flat rock about one hundred and fifty feet in diameter—jutted into the lake. One could fish inlet or lake with no impediments to casting, no submerged underbrush or reeds in which to entangle one's lure. On the second day in camp the household head persuaded his spouse to accompany him to the spot to fish. Once arrived, the kitchen head rummaged through the tackle box, selecting a small silver spinner. Considering that too dainty a lure for such a formidable creature as a lake trout, the household head chose a heavy three-inch spoon. While he was tying it on, the kitchen administrator made her second cast and hooked a twelve-inch rainbow. Apparently that was the only fish around the rock that day, however; after another hour of effortless but fruitless casting, the moderately successful fisherwoman grew bored, her frustrated companion grew depressed, and both returned to camp.

But the household head reasoned that where one trout had lingered, others must be lurking. Next morning he appropriated the lucky silver spinner for his own line and fished steadily from the rock for two hours without success. Thereafter he repeated the ritual daily, getting up earlier each morning, twice fishing past lunchtime. At first

. . . he fished Lake Superior nine successive days without getting even a strike. Two factors accounted for his dogged persistence: the beauty of the fishing spot and the success of other household members.

he used only the silver spinner; but as day succeeded fish-less day, he began experimenting wildly with plastic min-nows and worms, with spoons, spinners, crankbait, and jigs. Thus he labored six days without a nibble. On the seventh day he was again bested.

On this occasion Sheila administered the ego-bruising coup. As usual, the household head rose early, walked to the fingernail rock, and fished inlet and lake. Just as he was ready to give up, Sheila ambled out, rod in hand; so he agreed to fish another hour. It took Sheila just fifteen min-utes to catch her fish, a fifteen-inch rainbow that gave her a good five-minute tussle before she could bring it close enough for her father to net. Needless to say, he netted it with mixed feelings. Needless to say further, Sheila was using the silver spinner.

Somewhere in Lake Superior, deep in the water off the starboard side of the fingernail rock, there lies a silver spin-ner, unattached, and probably by now rusted brown. For two days following Sheila's catch, the household head hiked faithfully to the rock, where he spent the morning casting the silver spinner into the waters of Lake Superior and reeling in nothing. At the end of the second day he removed the silver spinner from his line and, casting it one last time into the waters of Lake Superior, returned to camp, dismantled his fishing rod, and decreed a morato-rium on fishing for the summer.

Actually, he should not have been so chagrined by the Neys fingernail fishing fiasco, since earlier that summer he had enjoyed his best fishing luck ever. Camped at Pratt Lake, on Michigan's Upper Peninsula, he fished the Two-Hearted River with his friend and fellow camper Bruce Curtis, netting three small brook trout. But that success was as nothing compared with his May expedition on the Little Manistee. On that occasion he hooked the largest of five rainbow trout caught that day and shared the excite-ment of netting his half of a nine-pound chinook salmon.

The five pounds of combined trout and salmon that the blower-up of fish lengths pulled from the Little Manistee River constituted the best bulk-fishing day in his family camping years. His second-best day was in 1969, his first fishing summer. Fishing the Chippewa River east of Hayward, Wisconsin, he hooked an evil-looking three-pound freshwater clam on a crappie jig. Obviously he did not know at the time that he was using a crappie jig, or he would not have used it—crappie being scarce in the Chippewa River. Then again, perhaps he would have used it since he could not distinguish a crappie from a carp at the time. Apparently the clam had even less intelligence, for it clearly tried to swallow the jig. Indeed, it did not seem unduly distressed at having been caught, but it resisted valiantly all efforts to make it release the lure.

Three pounds of clam constituted the household head's sole catch that summer. The outdoor kitchen head had slightly better success, primarily because she matched wits with a sunfish that was even dumber than the clam. Having noticed it lurking in some rocky shallows of the Chippewa, she teased it much as one might tease a cat with a string—dangling into the water above it a piece of cork, painted and feathered to resemble a bug. The sunfish was admirably bold and foolishly gullible. When the kitchen administrator twitched the lure, it darted from its hiding place under a rock. After a few feints, it struck, snagging its upper lip on one of the three tiny hooks. The kitchen angler hauled it in and summoned her spouse to unhook the monster. The household head complied, then, pronouncing it too small to keep, tossed it back into the shallows, whereupon it darted back under the rock. Thinking there might be larger fish in the vicinity, the kitchen administrator dropped the cork bug in again, only to attract and eventually snare the same fish. In the next half hour she caught the sunfish five times more and probably could have hooked it indefinitely had she not tired of the sport and retired to camp, leaving the fish to its fate. Without doubt, that sunfish was fated for disaster. Having bitten seven times at a tasteless piece of feathered cork; been bitten back each time; lifted out of the water; and mauled, dangled, and dropped, it apparently was incapa-

ble of recognizing that the environment might be dangerous.

The open air kitchen administrator used that same
green and yellow, feathered cork bug at Franklin Lake the
following week, although this time she caught the same
fish only once. On this occasion the household adults were
fishing from a boat, fifty yards from shore. After they had
fished for twenty minutes without a bite, the kitchen head
instructed her husband to troll. Although he tried to persuade her that fishing from an anchored boat was more
advantageous, she, in turn, pointed out they had been fishing from an anchored boat without success. So the household head reluctantly complied.

Now, neither member of the party had the dimmest
notion whether casting or trolling was the better way to
fish Franklin Lake in mid-July. The kitchen administrator
wanted to troll because she saw another boater trolling
and therefore assumed that to be the proper method of
fishing the lake. The household head opposed trolling because the rented boat had no trolling motor. Indeed, the
boat had no motor at all, the household head having
elected to rent oars because they were cheaper. Since his
family had voted four-to-one for a motor, the household
head was not currently popular enough to get elected to
anything. Therefore, he thought it inadvisable to protest
too loudly against rowing. Reeling in his bass buster, he
hauled anchor, grasped the oars, and set to.

The kitchen head lolled in the bow, letting out fifteen
feet of line. And once again the feathered bug proved irre-
sistible to an idiotic, eight-inch whiskered fish that broke
water in its eagerness to devour cork. Flushed with
success, the catfish queen again cast the cork bug upon
the waters and instructed the household head to resume
trolling. Fortunately other fish were not so easily deceived.
After forty-five nibbleless minutes the renter of cheap
boats was granted leave from his labors.

Over the years the outdoor kitchen head has proved to
be a relatively indifferent fisherwoman. If a half hour
elapses without a catch or at least a promising strike, she

is invariably willing to return to camp, sometimes insistent on doing so. Her lack of persistence has been at times a source of irritation to the household head, who stubbornly clings to the belief that, if one but fishes long enough, one must inevitably encounter a fish that is all washed up and ready for lunch. On this occasion, however, he was deeply thankful that his wife was quick to abandon her rod.

In the summer of 1983 the household adults had occasion to revisit Franklin Lake. Since by this time they numbered a canoe among their articles of camping gear, the household head did not have to make any agonizing decisions about whether or not to rent a motor. Prompted by nostalgia and curious to see whether Franklin Lake fish had increased in intelligence, he proposed to the kitchen head that they paddle across the lake, trolling the green and yellow, feathered cork bug. That the bug still remained in the tackle box after fourteen years provided mute but eloquent testimony to its ineffectuality. And so it proved on this occasion as well. Nothing struck at the cork, there apparently having been but that one stupid catfish in the lake. Once having reached the reed bed on the opposite shore, we tossed the cork bug into the tackle box and fished for perch with nightcrawlers.

For that is one thing we finally learned after fourteen years of sporadic fishing: for amateurs live bait works better. And it stands to reason that the real thing might more consistently attract real fish. A plastic worm may look like a nightcrawler, but it is not tasty. A real nightcrawler both looks and tastes like one—an assertion I make out of faith not fact, having tasted only those smaller cousins that dwell in apples. Except for an occasional clam or idiot sunfish, surely most aquatic creatures have taste buds of some sort.

Our disinclination to use live bait for so many years did not stem from squeamishness however. Although we are both reluctant to caress crickets or thread leeches, we never felt loathing for worms and minnows. Our penchant for artificial lures stemmed from beginner's luck in using such. Indeed, only our cooperative folly prevented our making a killing the first time out. We purchased our initial fishing gear in 1969 during our annual Easter-week trip to Table Rock Lake, Missouri. The next day we drove to a marina, rented a boat complete with motor, then returned to a cove near our campsite where we could fish while keeping an eye on our nonfishing children. About fifteen minutes after we started casting, a brief shower sprang up, following which the bass started striking. Within five minutes we caught four, losing a fifth when it slipped the hook while the kitchen head was lifting it into the boat.

That lost fifth fish proved disastrous. Instead of continuing to cast, we hauled in lines and motored back to the marina to buy a net. The round trip took nearly an hour, and by the time we returned to the cove, the school of bass had let out for recess. We caught no more bass that day. Indeed, five fishless years elapsed before the household head had need of the net to aid him in catching his 4½-pound portion of salmon.

Being without a net doubtless cost us a bass bonanza in 1969. For want of net and stringer the household head almost capsized a canoe in Flour Lake nine years later. That was 1978, the summer we shared the campground with the bears. Since the bears compelled our attention only at night, we had leisure to canoe and fish daytimes. Actually, the household head was the only licensed fisherman in the group that summer, so we primarily used the canoe for pleasure paddling. On some of these expeditions the household head would fish, but casually and without expectation. That explains why he left net and tackle box in camp on the occasion when he needed them.

Accompanied by Sheila, he paddled across the lake to explore the shoreline in search of a trail that purportedly led to an abandoned lumber camp. Father and daughter poked around for half an hour without locating the trail; then, before beginning the forty-five-minute paddle back to camp, they allowed the canoe to drift in the cove while the household head idly cast a spinner toward the shore. Almost immediately his rod tip kicked, following which, the drag began a gritty chatter. The fish headed first for the shallows, then, halted by drag pressure, doubled right and swam for open water; than it began to whipsaw. Twice the line went slack, causing the fisherman in the stern to fear his quarry had thrown the hook. But each time, reeling furiously, he managed to bring the struggle closer to the canoe. Once the fish dived directly under the canoe, forcing the household head to release the drag to keep the line from snapping.

It was the most violent fish fight he ever engaged in; but he took encouragement from Sheila, who sat in the bow excitedly cheering him on. All through the battle the stern fisherman alternately cursed the fish for its stubbornness and himself for having left the net in camp. Since the fish had not surfaced, he had no clear idea of its size. But its ferocity increased his fear that he would never be able to land it—or, more accurately, canoe it—without a net. Then the fish broke water for the first time, about six feet from the canoe. Seconds later the fisherman had a clear idea of the size of his catch *and* found his net problem solved.

For when the fish surfaced, it leaped directly into the canoe. One moment the household head was struggling to control his doubled rod; a moment later he was staring at a twenty-three-inch northern pike thrashing in the bottom of the canoe, up front, almost under his daughter's feet. Meanwhile Sheila continued her excited commentary. But now, his concentration no longer so singly devoted to the battle, the fisherman had opportunity to closely attend to her words.

"You're going to get us both killed," she shrieked. "You're going to drown us all!"

Apparently in the excitement of the struggle the household head had shifted his weight rather more abruptly and heavily than usual. Intent on his own troubles he had not noticed the canoe rocking to within inches of the water line. Or so Sheila claimed. But now, with only the northern thrashing, both the canoe and the Cassandra in the bow became more stable.

Since both paddlers were wearing life jackets, the household head tended to discount Sheila's assessment of the danger they had survived. While capsizing a canoe in Flour Lake's July waters might have led to discomfort, drowning and death seemed remote possibilities. Moreover, he was grieved at the unjustness of her accusations. After all, had the canoe truly capsized, it would clearly have been the northern's fault, not his.

Furthermore, he still had the thrashing northern to deal with. A northern that could leap into the canoe with such agility could as surely leap out. He needed somehow to subdue it without aid of stringer or filleting knife, both of which were in the missing tackle box. After a minute's thought, however, he realized he was not totally without arms. Suiting thought to action, he grasped his canoe paddle firmly in both hands and clubbed at the thrashing northern, while the canoe rocked and Sheila raged. Eventually he dispatched his foe; quieted his daughter; returned to camp; filleted the pike, fried, and ate it. It was quite tasty, although the flesh was a bit mushy around the bruise spots.

There were no bruise spots on either half of the chinook Bruce Curtis and the household head netted in May 1974. Nevertheless, it was a bruising battle waged by the nine-pound salmon against its would-be captors. For almost an hour the fishermen played the fish, wearing down its resistance until it could no longer avoid the net. And when finally they stumbled to shore, equally exhausted, water pouring from their badly slashed boots, they knew they had just concluded a truly memorable angling adventure.

The day began as a trout-fishing expedition on the Little Manistee River. The two companions put their canoe in at Nine Mile Bridge at eight-thirty, intent on floating the twelve miles to the weir, beaching the canoe frequently en route to fish inviting holes. About midmorning, after the second such beaching, they encountered the chinook.

At the time the household head was fishing a log-infested hole downstream from the beached canoe, while

Bruce had waded thirty or forty yards upstream, out of sight around a bend. To be precise, only Bruce was fishing. The downstream angler's first cast made contact with a log too large to reel in, in water too deep and cold to be reached by a current-clumsied novitiate wearing hip-length waders. So he cut the line, then, semiblind without his reading glasses, spent the next twenty minutes retying a hook, threading a nightcrawler, and cursing evenly under his breath.

A shrill command from upstream interrupted his meditations: "Stuart! Quick! Get your net." Puzzled by the command but eager to obey, the downstream fisherman laid his rod in the stern of the canoe, grabbed his net, and began sloshing upstream. Although he had not been instructed to leave his rod behind, it was well he did, for he had no need of traditional angling paraphernalia thereafter.

Moments after he shouted, Bruce appeared around the bend, rod waving in his right hand, while with his left he made scooping motions with his net. "There's a big chinook right ahead of me," he called. "If he gets to you, net him or try to turn him before he gets past into deep water."

Unlearned in the art of seining fish, the downstream fisherman heeded only the command to turn the salmon at the canoe. Having herded livestock in his youth and having watched grade B westerns all his life, he felt equal to that task. He waited—feet apart and planted firmly, knees slightly bent, arms relaxed and loosely flexed. When the chinook appeared, he shouted, stamped his feet, and rapped the fish smartly on the nose with his net. True to his expectation, the salmon wheeled and headed back upstream.

Only when the battle was nearly over did the household head learn how it began. While fishing the upstream pool, Bruce glanced down, his attention caught by a rippled shadow on the water. Upon closer scrutiny the ripple turned into a thirty-inch fish bearing down on him, seemingly intent on devouring his vital organ. Not until it began to glide harmlessly through his spread legs did he recover from paralysis of fear. Then he reacted with alacrity, clamped his knees together, and momentarily halted the salmon's forward progress. But before he could grasp its tail with his free hand, it wriggled loose—whereupon he pursued it, calling upon his downstream companion for aid.

Ultimately the chinook turned out to be neither malevolent nor especially mobile. It was, in fact, on its last fins. Having swum upstream from Lake Michigan to spawn, and prohibited by instinct from returning to the lake, it was hanging around, guarding its nest, waiting to die. Both fishermen were eager to administer last rites.

But the battle was far from over, the chinook having still sufficient agility to avoid the encroaching nets of its pursuers. For forty minutes the two would-be salmon-slayers thrashed over rocks and sloshed through the waist-high waters of the Little Manistee, angling for their quarry. That is, they sought to drive the chinook into the shallows where they might trap it in an angle of the bank. Unfortunately they too often had to slosh through deeper than waist-high waters in order to drive or turn the fish. Consequently their boots filled with water, making sloshing more difficult. Then, just as fish and fishermen were nearing total exhaustion, the canoe came unbeached.

Seeing the stern shift into the current preparatory to pulling the bow off the bank, the downstream fisherman shouted to his companion to slosh down and rescue it. By this time, due to the confusion and complexity of the chase, the downstream fisherman was located upstream of his Michigan partner. Thus was he afforded the opportunity of spotting the free-floating canoe and spared the grueling effort of trying to outslosh it. Being younger, more agile, and also owner of the canoe, Bruce proved adequate to the task of rescue. Fortunately the canoe turned sideways against the partially submerged log the household head had snagged earlier. Sloshing through water up to his armpits, Bruce retrieved the canoe and began towing it upstream. Meanwhile the downstream fisherman stood helplessly upstream, watching the chinook follow the canoe's owner downstream, finally to vanish in deep water.

The canoe safely rescued and the salmon apparently escaped, both fishermen stumbled ashore and removed their waders, thus refilling the Little Manistee. Having caught their breath and regained composure, they began to speculate about the lost chinook's probable size. It had been too large to net anyway, they agreed—probably forty inches, possibly over four feet. And losing the chinook was preferable to losing the canoe. Conversation shifted, and while the two discussed what they would have done had the canoe floated free, the salmon reappeared, slowly swimming upstream. With renewed hope the fishermen plunged off the bank, nets in hand.

First, however, they consulted on matters of strategy. Instead of trying to corner the chinook, they decided to flank it, moving only when necessary to turn the salmon and keep it swimming. Thus they hoped eventually to exhaust the fish without exhausting themselves. As a further precaution they slashed their waders at ankle height, reasoning that water pouring in at the top might find its way out the bottom.

Whether boot-slashing would have proved effective remains a mystery. In the battle's brief second round neither fisherman was forced into over-waist-high water. For ten minutes the chinook swam back and forth between its assailants, but ever more sluggishly, without side feints. Finally, Bruce, wading with the current, stalked it from behind, slipped his net under, dipped, and the battle was over.

Only after they had gutted and strung their catch did the fishermen begin to wonder if they had violated the law. Seining fish was illegal, they knew; but was an ordinary net considered a seine? What if a game warden should appear along the banks of the Little Manistee to ask how they caught the salmon? Since it is well known that chinook stop eating once they head upstream to spawn, they feared no warden would believe they had caught it with a nightcrawler or tie-fly. Expecting to fish only for trout, they had brought no large lures—no spoons, spinners, or buzz bugs that a salmon might conceivably regard as an enemy and attack. What explanation would disarm a suspicious warden?

The problem involved them the rest of the day while they floated down the Little Manistee. In the afternoon they netted five rainbows, meanwhile conspiring to fabricate a story that would reasonably account for their custody of a nine-pound chinook. Indeed, they became so enamored of their tale that they were disappointed when the day ended without a warden-encounter. But no matter, they agreed; their wives would be curious as to how they had caught the salmon. And their tale would be more safely told unofficially in the event they were not believed.

Accordingly, several hours later, while Joy Curtis fried salmon steaks by lantern light and the outdoor kitchen head chopped lettuce, onion, and green pepper, the two fishermen, faces carefully concealed in the shadows, launched their version of the battle of the Little Manistee.

"We got him at a trout hole just above Six Mile Bridge," Bruce said. "I had a rainbow hooked, putting up a heck of a fight. He must have zigzagged too close to the chinook's nest. Anyway, the chinook attacked, and the trout skittered across the stream into the shallows, under a log. The chinook went after it and wedged itself between the log and the rocks. I had to pull both of them out by hand."

There ensued a silence broken only by the sizzle of salmon steak in the skillet.

"And did they bite your little handsies?" Joy inquired.

"That's the way it happened," Bruce insisted, ignoring catcalls. "Wasn't it, Stuart?"

"It's the truth," the household head confirmed. Then remembering a clincher phrase from grade-school playground years, he added triumphantly, "You weren't there, so you can't prove it's not true."

"Who would want to try?" the outdoor kitchen head quartered a tomato. "And you expected a *game warden* to believe that story? Jason and T. J. could do better than that."

Unwilling to recant, the fishermen tried to steer the

conversation into other channels but without success. Scorn and scepticism put rational discourse to rout during dinner and throughout the evening.

Eventually the campfire burned low and the scorned fishermen retired, each accompanied by a sceptical spouse. As they undressed, the kitchen administrator reintroduced the subject on a less aggressive note. "It was a good story," she said. "But now you've had your fun, tell me what really happened."

It was a golden moment. And for once the blower-up of fishing accomplishments had anticipated it.

"You're right," he agreed. "Bruce made up that story. Fact is, he didn't catch the chinook; I did." He paused, then added, "I was using the green and yellow, feathered cork bug."

Thoroughly Unwalled

WHETHER OR NOT the perfect campsite exists is problematic. Of course, if the camper wants his "home away from home" to resemble the home he is away from, there are hundreds of state parks and KOA campgrounds which offer all the suburban conveniences—flush toilets, showers, electricity, treeless expanses, and friendly neighbors crowded close around. The more particular camper, seeking beauty, solitude, and recreational diversity—all in a relatively undisturbed natural habitat—will find his choices more limited.

For the Wenzel sidewall/Hettrick high wall/three-Eureka/Sears umbrella household identifying the ideal was complicated because its members had diverse preferences. T. J., for example, doted on sandy sites that provided unlimited opportunity for building roads on which to maneuver little cars. The adults viewed roads and little cars underfoot as a nuisance and sand as an abomination to be constantly swept from the tent. The open air kitchen administrator preferred coniferous forestation; the household head, deciduous. Sheila and Becky preferred lakeside sites; the adults, sites featuring rushing streams. In the very early years all the children would have welcomed a campground that had a Dairy Queen or Pizza Hut located at the front gate. But this was a juvenile ideal we were confident they would outgrow.

Small differences aside, we all agreed that an ideal campsite would include the following features: a spacious area surrounded by trees and brush screening the other sites; a level tent pad fronting a lake or stream, the lake with an expanse of sandy beach, both swarming with starving fish; an abundance of down timber for firewood; dozens of bird species flitting in the trees; lots of nonaggressive wildlife; all mosquitoes in permanent hibernation; constant shirt-sleeve, sunny weather. Finally, to be supremely perfect the campground should be unoccupied save for ourselves. While we never discovered a campground that met all the above criteria, we found many that supplied minimum essentials for ideal camping—privacy, swimming or fishing water, and forestation.

Over the years we became increasingly adept at identifying potentially ideal campgrounds. An invaluable aid to our efforts was *Campgrounds Unlimited*, a guidebook published in Longford, Kansas, now, unfortunately, out of print. In addition to an amazingly complete listing of campgrounds countrywide, the book supplied basic information regarding facilities and recreational features. With experience we learned to distinguish between what would be likely to attract others and what would prove satisfying for us.

Very early we discovered that national forest campgrounds are generally superior to those in state and national parks and those constructed by the Corps of Engineers. Engineers are fond of bulldozing, landscaping, and replanting. Some of their campgrounds will be beautiful in fifty years unless they are redecorated in the interim. State and national parks are quite appropriately designed for use by the public, campers and noncampers alike. Thus, the picnic grounds are often more scenic and spacious than the campgrounds. Campsites in such parks often resemble pastoral row houses. Vegetation is scant, privacy limited or nonexistent. Furthermore, a constant bustle of garbage and fee collectors produces an effect all too similar to the city activity one has gone camping to escape. Like universities, state and national parks tend to be top-heavy with superfluous administrative personnel whose main purpose is self-perpetuation through proliferation of paperwork. Invariably there are more posted rules in such campgrounds and more agents to enforce them. Supervisors supervise managers, managers manage rangers, and rangers range the campground seeking lackeys to order around; in turn the lackeys, lacking an underling to turn to, turn to the camper.

National forest campgrounds being generally understaffed, supervisors necessarily function as garbage-collectors, grass-cutters, and bathroom-cleaners. Having more real work to do, they are generally less officious. A national forest ranger is more likely to view the camper as a welcome guest, rather than as a nuisance underfoot.

By the same token Forest Service rangers are necessarily less responsive to the camper's needs. A tent camper choosing a small, isolated campground may find the garbage can full and smelly, the toilet paper dispenser jammed or empty. But that is the price of solitude—a small price easily paid. One can carry one's own toilet paper and squash the garbage with one's foot.

National forest campgrounds tend to be more spacious, vegetation more lush, trails less traveled. Another attractive feature involves the relaxation of rules regarding campfires. National parks prohibit cutting or gathering wood. Instead, they sell firewood—six or seven sticks of uncured birch or pine, which usually won't fit in the designed-for-charcoal fireplace. National forests permit gathering down wood. If one has an axe or saw and the energy to scavenge, one need never be without a fire. Most campers are subject to territorial limitations and partial to trails. They will walk a hundred yards along road or trail looking for wood and may even venture into the woods as much as forty feet. But a camper willing to brave poison ivy danger and careless of a few bramble scratches is almost certain to find firewood, even in the most frequented campgrounds.

By preference we were settlers. Finding a suitable campground, we tended to stay a week or more unless foul weather intervened. When we moved, we tried to locate a campground within five hours' driving distance—preferably a semideserted one. In researching our guidebook we looked for campgrounds located on gravel roads, fifteen miles or more from the nearest town, and featuring pit toilets—pavement and the propinquity of showers and supermarkets invariably attracting the comforts-of-home campers. Campgrounds offering only fishing and hiking as recreational attractions were generally not crowded. While we favored spots where swimming was available, we tried to avoid campgrounds with organized beaches.

In addition we discovered that a campground's size affects its popularity. An isolated campground with forty-five sites tends to fill more quickly than does a remote, ten-site campground. This was an important discovery, since it is no fun to drive five hours only to arrive at a filled campground. So we learned also to choose our moving day, avoiding Fridays and Saturdays, since the small isolated campgrounds tended to attract weekenders. By the same token, if we arrived at such campgrounds late Sunday afternoon, we usually had considerable choice of site.

We enjoyed many Sunday evening arrivals at deserted national forest campgrounds. On such occasions selecting a site and settling in became a romance of quietude. Locating bathrooms and the water pump were adventures to be undertaken at leisure. Indeed, leisure was the keynote of the hour. Dinner tastes better in a deserted campground. Trees have more individuality, loop roads more distance, night sounds more vibrance. Among the campgrounds on our "nearly ideal" list, many we had to ourselves.

Teton Wilderness Salt Lick Cow Pie is an example. In 1968 we planned a three-week camping trip with Bruce and Joy Curtis, beginning with a rendezvous at Jenny

Lake, a campground in Teton National Park. Given the crowded conditions at national parks, the row-house congestion of the campsites, it was a bad spot for a rendezvous. But this being only our second year of summer camping, we had not yet learned to interpret our guidebook.

We arrived at Jenny Lake in midmorning, two days ahead of schedule, hoping to reserve an adjacent site for Bruce and Joy by paying for the vacancy in the interim. A patronizing gate attendant informed us that the campground had been filled since nine. If we wanted to camp at Jenny Lake, we would need to come back the next day and wait in line. If we arrived gateside by five, we might get in. A ranger would assign us a site, matching available sites against the size of our tent. Reserving an adjacent site for someone else was out of the question.

Disbelieving, we drove the loop road anyway, certain there must be vacant sites so early in the day. But the campground was indeed full—jammed full, in fact, with men, women, tents, trailers, cars, children, and dogs. Furthermore, the sites were tiny and cramped. Had we found an empty tent pad on which to erect our ten-by-sixteen Hettrick high wall, we would have assuredly crushed a child or dog. Jenny Lake may be an attractive campground; our first and only impression was that it needed only a company store in order to fully resemble a migrant workers' camp.

Unwilling to wait hours in line for a possible ranger-appointed campsite, we abandoned all plans to meet Bruce and Joy in Teton National Park. But since we had failed to designate an alternate rendezvous spot, we found ourselves in a quandary, not knowing what our next step should be. Our frustrations paled beside the children's indignation at having another "there yet" thrust upon them in a single day. All traveling parents have had the experience: one starts a day-long journey at sunrise; by eight the children are asking, "Are we there yet?" In the present case the situation was further aggravated. We had told Sheila, Becky, and T. J. that we were going to camp at Jenny Lake; we had arrived at Jenny Lake; now we were leaving Jenny Lake, adults in a foul mood made fouler by backseat demonstrations of disappointment.

Twenty miles east on Highway 26 we stopped for lunch at a roadside table. While munching salami sandwiches and potato chips, we pored over map and guidebook looking for a stopgap campground nearby. In the midst of our research we took belated note of a ranger station across the road and, behind it, a fire road leading into the Teton Wilderness. "I'll bet it wouldn't be crowded up there," the household head observed. Then, more excitedly, "Do you suppose they'd let us?"

After discussing the prospect, we crossed the road, accosted the ranger, and requested permission to pitch a primitive wilderness camp. Surprisingly, he consented, exacting from us only a promise to return and mark our campsite location on his wall map. Accordingly, we drove cautiously up the winding, rocky road, located a suitable spot twelve miles in, and began a week of primitive camping.

Teton Wilderness Salt Lick Cow Pie was a site cleared, occupied, and decorated by range cattle—although it was not currently in use. Except for the hundreds of sun-dried cow pies scattered around, the spot looked ready for immediate occupancy. So, prior to unloading, we taught the children the art of frisbee-sailing. Within minutes Sheila, Becky, and T. J. cleared space for tent and kitchen; within an hour we were settled in.

The site had minor drawbacks, being slightly cluttered with fallen trees and still unfrisbeed cow pies. But in addition to the novelty of the experience several factors contributed to making the range cattle salt lick a nearly ideal campsite. To the west lay an unbroken expanse of forest—towering white pines intermixed with a tangle of second-growth pine and down timber, beyond which loomed the 10,300-foot peak of Mt. Leidy. To the east lay a meadow brilliant with wildflowers—a Cezanne landscape framed by fire road and distant treeline. A mountain rivulet, two feet wide and almost as deep, wound through the meadow. It was a splendid area, which we shared only with the mule deer daytimes and the coyotes at night.

For once our luxury equipment proved useful. We hung the lantern on the lantern pole; the short-legged card table served as something more than a depository for clutter. We arranged homemade pine-log stools around our brown box boxtop table and dined with elegance and ease.

We converted the mountain stream into a refrigerator. Cutting wooden stakes and driving them into the pebbled stream bed, we fashioned a sluice dam to contain and cool our perishables. Beer, pop, milk, juice, mayonnaise—all tasted better for having been cooled in the stream's rushing current. Or, rather, most of the pop and beer tasted better. On the morning after arrival the household head volunteered to hike for orange juice. Walking to the dam, he found but half a dam, the rushing current having eroded the banks to the sides of the stakes. Milk and mayonnaise remained, held by flow pressure to the center of the sluice. But a dozen cans of beer and pop had whirled with the current around the eroded sides.

We initiated a downstream search and eventually recovered a few cans that had lodged against the roots of a shrub growing out of the bank. The rest were irretrievably gone, a tragedy which prompted the household head to guzzle two quick beers, thus forestalling further loss. At this point the kitchen administrator intervened, suggesting further tragedy might be averted by construction of a backup dam. Having accomplished this, we thereafter checked the primary dam frequently, and always at sunset. When it weakened, we dismantled it, reconstructing it as backup sluice downstream. By the week's end we were walking farther for milk and beer, but we suffered no more losses of vital foodstuffs.

Having solved our dam problems, we drove to Jenny Lake, left instructions for the Curtises on the campground message board, purchased a grubstake in Jackson, and returned to Teton Wilderness Salt Lick Cow Pie. Bruce, Joy, Hilary, and Jason joined us the next day, and we spent five additional delightful days before the mosquitoes drove us out.

It was a week of adventure and creativity. Bruce and

the household head hiked to the summit of Mt. Leidy,
thereby making some valuable discoveries about mountain climbing. Primarily we discovered that summits are
never as close as they look. Because Mt. Leidy loomed so
imposingly over our campsite, it appeared we could reach
the top by attacking it frontally. For two hours we clawed
and crawled our way up a glacial wash. When we finally
scrambled out of this declivity, we discovered that our
campsite view of the summit had been obscured by the
cliff face we had just scaled. The summit loomed ahead, to
the right. We trudged upward, repeatedly sighting a
"peak" that turned into a plateau that had obscured the
real summit. Three hours after we scrambled out of the
wash, we finally reached a meadow from which the terrain
sloped downward in every direction. We had expected tun-
dra but were rewarded with fireweed and Indian
paintbrush instead. Even the three-hour steady rain attending our descent failed to dampen our spirits. We encountered several herds of mule deer, walked a weeks-old
fawn out of its lair, and arrived back in camp, wet and cold
but exhilarated by the day's experience.

Mountain climbing was but one of several diversions.
Among its luxury items the party numbered horseshoes, a
croquet set, and jarts—games made more exciting by cow-
pie impediments. We took numerous hikes, played frisbee
football (with a real frisbee), and at mealtimes watched the
Stellar's jays that flocked in to gorge on table scraps.

A mile or so south in a clearing visible from the road
lay a dead range cow. From our campsite we watched the
vultures patiently circling above it. Once, driving the road,
we saw a half-dozen vultures hunched in the clearing,
staring at the carcass, while a raven perched atop it, a
black-robed auctioneer ready to gavel down dinner to the
highest bidder.

On the fourth day our solitude was temporarily interrupted. About lunchtime a battered pickup, complete with
antler-fashioned gun rack behind the cab, bucked up the
fire road, halting by our site. When we saw the driver, we
understood why the vehicle had been bucking. From head

to foot he was the archetypal cowboy: white sombrero shading a wonderfully lined and weather-beaten face, black and red flannel shirt tucked into broadly belted and faded jeans, fawn-colored boots with sharply pointed toes—and spurs. In one detail only did he lapse from the ideal. A grizzled Bopeep of the Tetons, he had apparently lost his cows. Spurs a-jangle, he strode into our site and stretched his hands out over our campfire. "Howdy folks," he said. "Saw the smoke from your fire quite a ways down the road. That old dead pine sure does burn dirty. Doin' a little camping, are you?"

Not knowing whether he had intentionally insulted our fire or not, we confined ourselves to the admission that we had been doing a little camping.

"The ranger said you've been up here three or four days," he said. "Have you seen any white-faced cattle since you been up here?"

We told him no and were immediately corrected by the children, who excitedly told him about the dead Hereford down the road, about the vultures, about how bad the clearing smelled, about . . .

Archetypal cowboy appeared to be unimpressed with this information. "I kinda thought they'd be grazing in the meadow, yonder," he said. "Maybe you spooked them. They're kinda skittish around people." He tipped his hat. "Well, they gotta be uptrail somewheres." Striding back to his pickup, he revved the engine, dug his spurs into the foot feed, and disappeared, riding his steel-belted cayuse uptrail through the purple sage.

For our part we were thankful not to have to share the meadow, range cattle tending to be somewhat disruptive of solitude and serenity. And the prospect of drinking from the same cup with several hundred Herefords did not appeal. In short, we preferred our rivulet unmuddied, our meadow ungarnished and ungrazed.

For ultimately it is the mountain rivulet that orders our mind's eye image of Teton Wilderness Salt Lick Cow Pie. Although Sheila was only seven that summer, Becky four, and T. J. just shy of three, all have vivid recollections of the spot. T. J. remembers standing in the icy stream, helping pound sluice stakes; Sheila and Becky recall fetching wash and drinking water daily; both adults remember the brilliantly blooming meadow through which the rivulet wound; everyone remembers the two-hour downstream search for the current-wafted Coors.

Indeed, our pleasant recollection of numerous campsites stems from the circumstance of a stream that lulled us to sleep nights. Thus do we recall Huzzah Creek, a campground near Davisville, Missouri, where we spent the first week of our 1972 vacation. Water flowing over the Huzzah's rock bottom was absolutely limpid. We swam in the creek, fished it, drank from it. Someone had detached an inch-thick creeping vine from its roots so that it dangled, suspended from a gnarled white oak limb, over the swimming hole. The children spent hours swinging back and forth across the stream or, more courageously, dropping in midswing into the deepest water. A kingbird nesting nearby daily harassed a green heron that fished the shore too close to its nest. A dead elm on the hillside across the stream served as drumming tree for numerous pileated woodpeckers. Wood was plentiful, though much of it required splitting. Thus, when the household head discovered a double-bitted axe with a pre–World War II price tag in the Davisville general store, his joy in the campground was compounded. A crackling fire on the bank of a coursing stream makes an almost unbeatable combination.

Memory of a flowing stream can soften or obliterate other circumstances less pleasant to recall. In 1975 we drove for eight hours, east through Illinois into Indiana, in a rainstorm so intense that it penetrated the canvas bag atop the Ford wagon, soaking all equipment within. Arriving late at Morgan Monroe Campground in Brown County State Forest, we sat in the wagon two additional hours, waiting for the storm to subside. Eventually we despaired and pitched our three Eurekas by lantern light in the driving rain, thus soaking our remaining dry clothes. About nine-thirty, wet, cold, and bedraggled, we drove to a laundromat in Martinsville, eating a forgettable cheese sandwich dinner while drying in shifts all the clothing we had brought on the trip. But when finally we returned to camp with our coin-dried clothes and sleeping bags, we slept snugly with the sound of the stream's rain-swollen current in our ears.

Morgan Monroe was a veritable bird haven. During our four-day stay we sighted fifty-nine species, most of them within the campsite environs. A summer tanager literally invaded our site while we breakfasted one morning, lighting on the table to steal our bacon. A trail led to a fire lookout tower; and Sheila, Becky, and T. J. were all old enough to climb it alone. Evenings the household members engaged in bitterly contested games of hearts. Nightly the stream sang us to sleep. Despite that awful first night Morgan Monroe ranks high on our list of ideal campgrounds.

Three weeks later we pitched camp by lantern light again, at Greendale, a Green Mountain National Forest campground near Ludlow, Vermont. In this instance we violated our principle of locating a campground within five hours' driving distance. Having visited a few days with Ruth and J. R. Fawley, we left Norristown, Pennsylvania, intent on driving to New England nonstop. Trying to avoid the congested seaboard area, we kept veering west, consequently making slow progress. Still, we would have reached Greendale in a long day's journey, rather than a long day's journey into night, had the household head read the map properly.

The journey began inauspiciously. As the party poked through the Poconos, the navigator–household head identified Greendale as a likely site to head for. Although our guidebook listed no special recreational facilities, it did note that "campsites in this forest are generally too small for travel trailers," a clue suggesting an isolated, possibly ideal campground. Unfortunately, in reading the literature the household head misread the directions. At a crucial juncture he steered the party east on Highway 9 toward

Brattleboro. Somewhere along that route he belatedly became aware that Ludlow was seventy miles north, accessible most easily by a highway already bypassed at the crucial juncture.

Fortunately the kitchen administrator was in a benevolent mood. Instead of calling the navigator an ignoramus, she suggested that the party halt, eat dinner roadside, then backtrack, arriving "whenever we get there." Accordingly, we pulled off at a spot where the Deerfield River was visible from the shoulder, and the outdoor kitchen head prepared a stove-top casserole of sausage sizzlers and beans. A tossed salad plus thick slices of french bread turned the impromptu meal into a feast, richly laid out on the Ford's lowered tailgate. We ate standing but without haste, our only concession to expedience being that we left the dishes unwashed. Our itinerary having gotten screwed up, we determined not to let the screwup screw up our day.

Sometime before midnight we arrived at Greendale to find the campground full. But, our sense of adventure sustaining us, we pitched an illegal, makeshift camp in the picnic grounds. Normal turnover left several sites vacant the next morning. We circled the loop and were welcomed into a small, picturesque streamside site by a small, vociferous winter wren. That the wren's tinkling song was so clearly audible attests to the campground's quietude. Although the fish were too small to bother with, the stream sparkled and gamboled over its rocky bottom. Feeling destination-driven, we stayed only three days. But we truly intend to return to Greendale—to wade the stream, fish for the now-grown trout, and to enjoy, evenings, the chimelike serenade of the resident wren.

The greatest of all rushing stream sites was Muffler Creek, in Utah's Manti-Lasal National Forest. We discovered it in 1970. Seeking a remote campground, we drove into the mountains, then somewhere en route took a wrong turn and found ourselves on a rocky, rain-rutted road that apparently went nowhere except serpentinely up. We bumped upward for an hour or so until the six-cylinder, overloaded Plymouth stalled on the eighty-seventh switchback. The stall proved climactic to the out-door kitchen head, the Plymouth's driver. "Do you still want to go on?" she said.

The household head, skilled at ferreting out symbolic meaning in literal speech, in this instance recognized a commandment lurking beneath the question's surface. Furthermore, he had been impressed with the camping possibilities of an area the party passed twenty minutes before. He would have recommended it then had he not been otherwise occupied, gritting his teeth and gripping the door above the rolled-down window. But now he suggested a return to the spot. His suggestion was readily, but not speedily, acted upon. Turning a station wagon on a hairpin curve that has earned its name from the angle of the turn *and* from the width of the road requires time. Moreover, descending the road proved more nerve-wracking than climbing it. When we finally emergency-braked the Plymouth on the road shoulder, carried our equipment across the creek, and pitched camp, we were ready for an extended stay.

We christened both campsite and stream. Though the latter probably has a name, we never found it on a map—primarily because we never knew precisely where we were. The campsite was located on a level knoll between the confluence of a rivulet and a larger mountain stream. A rusted muffler plus several stones bridged the rivulet—hence the name Muffler Creek. Clearly it was a site that campers and fishermen had used before.

Indeed, if ever we return to Muffler Creek, the household head will certainly carry a Utah fishing license. Muffler Creek's water ran so clear one could see multitudes of trout—hungry rainbows that lunged after the silhouette of stick and string dangled over the water. A reasonably law-abiding citizen, the household head was never so sorely beset by temptation as in this instance. Trout begged to be bagged. Grasshoppers abounded. Trout flies dangled from tree limbs shading the creek, mementoes of fishermen who had miscast.

He was persuaded from sin by the presence of a trailer located upstream, pulled by a Jeep which, according to lettered insignia, belonged to a deputy sheriff. Subsequent events suggested that the sheriff may have been a sinner also. On the third morning he waded out of the mountain stream into our campsite. "Do you like fish?" he graveled.

Having been for two days guilty in thought if not in deed, the household head mistook the phrase for "Doing any fishing?" and promptly denied having broken the law.

"I don't care about that," the deputy rasped. "I've already got more fish than we can use. Do you want these?" He held out his creel containing seven trout, all nicely cleaned.

We thanked him, dumped our half-cooked oatmeal, and breakfasted on trout—then spent the rest of the day pondering whether the deputy really didn't care if we broke the law.

Although ultimately we did no fishing, we found Muffler Creek so enchanting that we stayed until our supplies ran out. There were compensations for the lack of organized recreation. Since we had pitched the Hettrick within two feet of the stream, water sounds accompanied our every activity, day and night. The mountain stream was deep enough for swimming, providing one could withstand cold temperature and the assault of hungry trout. Raspberries being ripe, each day we gathered our evening's dessert. The adults spent numerous hours relaxed in chairs, binoculars in hand—an exercise rewarded one afternoon when several hundred kestrels kited on the clearing between our campsite and the switchback above. Was that the third or the fourth day? We do not remember. Having decided to stay for so long as supplies lasted, we had no deadline to meet. Being out of time, we had all the time we needed for whatever we wanted to do.

Indeed, over the years we learned that "planned time" often diminishes camping comfort. Doing without a watch entirely may be self-conscious and show-offish. Nevertheless, planning one's time too carefully often leads to frustration over uncompleted projects or to destination-oriented travel necessitating one-night stands at campgrounds where one would, in retrospect, rather have stayed longer.

Crocker Pond, near Bethel, Maine, is an example. Intent on reaching Acadia National Park, we camped at Crocker for a single night in 1969. The following winter over dinner-table reminiscence we discovered that the entire household harbored fond memories of Crocker Pond. We vowed, therefore, that should the opportunity arise, we would return and spend several days. Six years later we spent a peaceful week at Crocker Pond.

Crocker Pond is primarily memorable for its isolation, its boulders, its bullfrogs, and its bathrooms. Each of the seven sites is widely separated from the rest by trees, boulders, and the curvature of the road. On both occasions we managed to secure the best site—a rock-strewn carry-in area secluded from the road, overlooking the pond. In 1969 bullfrogs held a convention at the site. Deprived of pets by parental decree, Sheila, Becky, and T. J. began capturing the frogs, imprisoning them in the largest of the cooking pots. To avoid a can-we-keep-them confrontation the household head shrewdly recounted Mark Twain's saga of the Calaveras County jumping contest. Frog racing immediately became a popular diversion, though the frogs' refusal to cooperate dampened festivities somewhat. Unweighted with buckshot, still they scrunched and squatted, apparently preferring captivity to exertion. Had the children not prodded them with sticks they would doubtless not have moved at all. After dark, however, they became more active, laying hoarse vocal claim to their territory—Croaker Pond.

Even on gray days Crocker Pond's shoreline was doubled—upside-down trees pushing clouds out into the middle of the pond. Loons and kingfishers patrolled the water daily and discussed their success, the former yodeling, the latter rattling. Save for their calls and the nightly crescendo of frogs, Crocker Pond was a model of quietude.

Only an occasional bang of a distant bathroom door interrupted the silence.

Crocker Pond had two bathrooms, one at each end of
the campground, both desegregated. One bathroom for
both sexes is an accepted tradition in American homes.
Only at Crocker Pond, however, did we find the concept
sensibly applied outdoors.

Loons and kingfishers excepted, the above description
is primarily derived from our 1969 one-night stand. Our
second visit was gratifying but not because it was
startlingly different. Except for there being fewer frogs, we
found the campground unchanged. It lived up to our memory of its attractions—a peaceful spot, a place where one
might relax, ignoring time.

Indeed, in our household conversations "the place
where" is an essential phrase identifying campgrounds we
nostalgically recall. Thus, Pog Lake, Ontario, is the place
where Sheila learned to swim, where Dad almost sawed his
thumb off, where multicolored mushrooms landscaped
our campsite. Grand Mesa, Colorado, is the place where
chipmunks invaded our tent, teaching us not to leave
peanuts inside. Big Bay Campground, at Table Rock Lake,
Missouri, is the place where we held Easter egg hunts
every spring, where we found the chunk of petrified cedar
along the lakeshore, and where we pitched camp on snow
in 1970. Beaver Meadows Campground, Pennsylvania,
T. J.'s all-time favorite, is the place where each site had
access to a baseball field–sized playground. Bayview, on
Michigan's Lake Superior shore, is the place where we
built sand castles at low tide, then gathered hours later to
see whose pebble man would be the last to wash from the
ramparts into the deep. Tom Hannah, in Colorado, is the
place where black-chinned hummingbirds perched on our
fingers while drinking sugar water from a paper cup,
where our dog wore her pads bloody chasing chipmunks
over stony soil.

In 1970 at Gunnison, a campground on the rim of the
Black Canyon, T. J. constructed hundreds of feet of little-

car roadway out of white pine scrap-lumber firewood. In 1975 Becky went sleepwalking through Wildwood Campground in New Hampshire. Rescued by a neighboring camper, she kept the escapade a secret for several years. At Teton Canyon, Wyoming, in 1968 Sheila found a lucky horseshoe under a cattle guard, Becky found a set of antlers along a trail, and T. J. found the ground too wet for road construction. At Acadia National Park in 1969 Sheila lost her birthday jackknife while hiking around Jordan Pond. At Cumberland Gap in 1972 Becky lost out on a good birthday when the boughten cake tasted stale. At Lake Charles, Arkansas, in 1967 T. J. lost his bearings chasing a stray camp dog and became, himself, the object of a half hour's search.

In retrospect, it becomes clear that much of our memorable camping was distinguished by unimportant events. At Shenandoah National Park, the first summer, we took a ranger-led hike each day and attended the campground nature program every evening. Today we primarily remember the skunks that pestered us at dinnertime. During our two-week stay at Olive Ridge in 1970 we commuted daily to Rocky Mountain National Park to sample its attractions—trails, evening programs, scenic drives. Years later we chiefly remember the coyote that raced our Plymouth as we drove to the park, or we recall the broad-tailed hummingbirds that buzzed into our campsite to assault our red lantern or saw.

Both of these campgrounds had attractive sites, both experiences were pleasant. But seldom do we wax nostalgic about either place—probably because on both occasions we spent too much time having fun to the exclusion of more leisured activities. Pitching the tent; cooking dinner; gathering, sawing, and splitting wood; washing dishes; blowing up air mattresses; building a fire—these tasks are the essence of camping. As soon as they become chores to be accomplished in order to have time for fun, most of the fun is lost. All household members agree that one of our finest campsites was in the Ouachita National Forest, in Arkansas. Invariably we refer to it as the place where we hand-carried our gear across the loop road to relocate in a streamside site. No one remembers the campground's name—Shady Lake—unless we look it up in the guidebook. Nor do we recall specifics about the campground itself. We recall that our site was shaded, that the stream gurgled, that the swimming beach was a minute's walk away, that the lake water was warm. There was no sand for little-car roads, we recall; nor was there a Pizza Hut at the front gate. The gateside Pizza Hut was at Cross Lake, in Minnesota—a tolerable but not memorable campground.

A May-littered puppy accompanied us on our Arkansas trip, so a number of our recollections of Shady Lake are dog related. Neighboring campers pampered her outrageously, bringing her steak and chicken bones and, once, almost five pounds of darkened hamburger that we thought seriously of using ourselves. One night, terrified by a possum that skulked through our site, Thor whimpered to be admitted into the tent, where she would be safe. On another night, she barked incessantly, protecting us from plastic-covered motorcycles parked in the adjacent campsite.

Sometime about the middle of our stay at Shady Lake, Sheila, Becky, and the household head packed overnight into a nearby wilderness area. Fish nibbled our fingers when we dipped water from the stream fronting our campsite; great horned, barred, and screech owls cacophonated until well past midnight; a morning fog put a last touch of perfection on the experience.

That is the only organized activity we recall. So what did we do the other twelve days? It was hot in Arkansas that summer, so we doubtless spent many hours swimming. We fished—without success, apparently—and probably did some casual hiking. Ultimately, however, what we remember is that we carried our equipment across the road, set up near a gurgling stream, and enjoyed ourselves for two weeks. It appears we must have relished the weather, the wildlife, the warm water, lots of relaxation, and each other.

That is ideal camping.